Acclaim for Star Parker's
Uncle Sam's Plantation

Daniel Patrick Moynihan's identification, in 1965, of the self-destructive roots of the Welfare State was prophetic. Star Parker's new book seizes on this theme, adds her personal sense of "been there and done that," and casts new light on the redemptive power of freedom.

RUSH LIMBAUGH

In *Uncle Sam's Plantation*, Star Parker has written her declaration of independence from the grand illusions, slippery safety nets, and moral muddles of the Welfare State. In this compelling and inspirational book, she presents a devastating critique of the socialist plans of the welfare bureaucrats and blasts into orbit her fireworks of faith, family, and freedom like an angelic avenger.

GEORGE GILDER,
fellow of the Discovery Institute and author of
Wealth and Poverty and *Men and Marriage.*

Star Parker's new book brings us back to eternal truths—faith, family, love, and responsibility.

DR. LAURA SCHLESSINGER,
syndicated radio host and author of the *New York Times* bestseller,
Ten Stupid Things Couples Do To Mess Up Their Relationships

Star Parker's important new book helps advance the understanding—critical for all Americans—that prosperity does not come from government and politics but results from men and women of character and high moral fiber living and working in freedom.

LARRY KUDLOW,
economist, author, and co-host of CNBC's *Kudlow and Cramer*

I have known Star Parker for almost twenty years. Her background gives her the experience to challenge us to get off the fence and get involved in creating a better society for all. I admire her for speaking up and expressing her fresh and compelling ideas. She is not striving to be popular; she is striving to be right. We all should be open to read and to learn from *Uncle Sam's Plantation.*

ROSEY GRIER,
football great, author, activist, humanitarian, and board member of
the Milken Family Foundation

Star Parker rocks the world. She is an iconoclast that must be listened to and reckoned with.

SEAN HANNITY,
syndicated radio host and co-host of Fox News's *Hannity & Colmes*

Lots of tomes make theoretical points about welfare. This shooting star of a book shows the doleful experiences and one gutsy woman's reaction to them. Look elsewhere for sociological accounts. Look here for the emotions of plantation life and escape.

MARVIN OLASKY,
editor-in-chief of *World Magazine* and author of
The Tragedy of American Compassion

The title of Star Parker's new book says it all. For a clear, balanced, and fair insight into the true nature and history of America's Welfare-State dabbling—and its effect upon those whom it is supposed to help—read this incisive and brilliant analysis of the problem by one who understands it through years of personal experience and dedicated study.

DR. D. JAMES KENNEDY,
pastor, author, and president of Coral Ridge Ministries

Like the North Star and Harriet Tubman, Star Parker is a living beacon to guide others to the freedom denied them by those who thrive on the backs of poor folks.

REV. JOHNNY M. HUNTER, DD,
president of Life Education and Resource Network
in Fayetteville, North Carolina

Star Parker's new book about the folly of government is an eye-opener. Her work to help improve the lives of ordinary women, men, and families who need a hand-up rather than a hand-out is exemplary.

DR. JULUETTE BARTLETT PACK,
executive director of Family Assistance Center in Houston, Texas

Every day, those of us who work in the trenches in Pregnancy Care Centers see the impact of the welfare system on the young women we serve. Thank God for Star's courage and insight as she eloquently puts words to what we face every day. I wish every one of our clients could have one hour with Star. Our work would be a lot easier!

DINAH MONAHAN,
founder and executive director of
Hope House Maternity Home in Show Low, Arizona

UNCLE SAM'S PLANTATION

HOW BIG GOVERNMENT
ENSLAVES AMERICA'S POOR *and* WHAT
WE CAN DO ABOUT IT

STAR PARKER

THOMAS NELSON
Since 1798

NASHVILLE   DALLAS   MEXICO CITY   RIO DE JANEIRO

Copyright © 2003 by Star Parker

Published in Nashville, Tennessee, by Thomas Nelson. Thomas Nelson is a registered trademark of Thomas Nelson, Inc.

Thomas Nelson, Inc. titles may be purchased in bulk for educational, business, fund-raising, or sales promotional use. For information, please e-mail SpecialMarkets@ThomasNelson.com.

Library of Congress Cataloging-in-Publication Data

Parker, Star.
    Uncle Sam's plantation : how big government enslaves America's poor and what we can do about it / Star Parker.
        p. cm.
    ISBN 0-7852-6219-9 (HC)
    ISBN 1-59555-015-1 (SC)
    1. Poor—Government policy—United States. 2. Public welfare—United States. 3. Dependency (Psychology) 4. Liberalism—United States. 5. Conservatism—United States. 6. African Americans—Social conditions. I. Title.
    HV95.P35 2003
    362.5'561'0973—dc22

                                                                    2003018893

Printed in the United States of America

HB 02.02.2018

*Dedicated in loving memory of
Gina (1968-2002) and Jonah (1989-2002)—
whose short yet spirited dashes on earth
symbolized hope for the poor.*

And to my Rachel Sarah . . .

Contents

1

What Is Poverty?

It was a hot and sticky 1968 summer evening in South Carolina. The only breeze was the air coming through the car windows. But as we traveled down the narrow street that led to Grandma Warreno's house, it was not the heat or the humidity that had me in a tizzy. I hated visiting my grandma's house; hated the old porch with posts so rotten it looked as if it would fall over at any moment; hated the cardboard nailed up to cover the holes in the wall. Lord knows how much I hated using that outhouse toilet. The only running water was in the kitchen, so we bathed in the backyard with the chickens, the spiders, and the mosquitoes.

Saying times were tough does not begin to describe my dad's life growing up. My grandpa died at a young age, leaving six adolescent sons to grow up in the Jim Crow segregated South with their widowed mother. It must not have occurred to my grandma that she needed any-one to alleviate her condition as she struggled to raise her boys without a husband and without complaint. Grandma pressed on without a dime from welfare. She grew her own food, trained her own kids, and paid her own way. All six grew to become professional and accomplished men.

It was not until Grandma Warreno was seventy-five years old that she looked to the government for help. She had been contributing Social Security and Medicare taxes all her working life believing the political promise that her retirement and medical needs would be met. That is when she discovered that the government did not do a very good job saving her money. The Social Security check she received was barely enough to retain the financial independence she struggled sixty-nine years to maintain. After her third stroke by age eighty-three, Medicaid put a lien on her four-thousand-dollar home to cover the housing expenses of the substandard nursing facility they had guaranteed.

What is poverty? It seems a simple question on the surface. People think they know it when they see it. Yet ask any politician, religious leader, or even one who considers himself poor to define poverty, and you will receive a variety of responses. Every time I visit the Union Rescue Mission in downtown Los Angeles, I wonder if the folks there are the picture that most people see when asked to define poverty. Homeless men covered with filth, their clothes soiled and bedraggled, the smell of any one of them enough to make your eyes water. Corporately the stench is not breathable.

Maybe the picture of poverty is the daily routine a few blocks away from the mission, where postal workers fear for their lives to deliver welfare checks, and two-year-olds roam the halls of run-down, hour-rate motels. Wearing diapers as dirty as the garbage in the alley where they play, they giggle as they chase rats while Mom is making a drug buy or meeting her next trick.

Are the political pundits, scholars, and think tanks of today talking about my grandmother or the street hustlers when they pontificate on how to alleviate poverty? Which poor are we discussing in the halls of Congress, Ivy League colleges, or multimillion-dollar churches? A paralytic? A drug addict? Or perhaps folks like my mom and dad?

Dad worked hard to provide for his wife and five children on a military paycheck. After twenty years of air force service, Dad retired, completed a master's degree in education, and taught elementary school until cancer disabled him ten years before his death at age sixty-nine. Mom spent her working life as a domestic, hairdresser, seamstress, correctional facility house parent, and now, at age seventy-two, a horticulturist for an exporter of seasonal flowers. Standing barely five feet tall, Mother, as she demanded us five children address her, is the most financially content person I know. She has never made more than ten bucks an hour. Yet when I talk with her about political debates over a government-mandated livable wage, she laughs and says that people ought not complain about whatever they get. I think her attitude reflects the fact that my mom really enjoys the creative freedom she finds working for small business owners, and she knows that they cannot pay a lot.

One of nine children, my mother learned as a "young'un" that, more than anything else, poverty is a state of mind. Her father showed her by example how to live free. "Buy property and a gun" was his edict. His faith and convictions told him free men have a right to own property and to protect it. Only one generation from slavery, my granddaddy bought enough land in 1905 that today all of his children and grandchildren can retire in Traveler's Rest, South Carolina, without a mortgage. My personal lot is two and a half acres.

My mom's upbringing conditioned her to believe people should be free to live as they choose without imposed restraints. At age sixty-nine, when she found out that in order to collect Social Security she would have to cut her work hours to part-time, she was furious. To recover the Social Security payroll taxes the government had been taking from every one of her paychecks for the last fifty years, they could dictate when and how much she would work? "Oh no they won't," she threatened once. "I'll vote Republican!"

Discovering that her retirement came with a heavy price tag in the form of government control was a real slap in the face. She would genuinely miss her work. I had seen how my mom's countenance would brighten during snowy New Jersey winters as she looked upon the thousands of poinsettia plants her tender loving care had nurtured. The plants were ready for the grand moment of shipping all across the state. They would arrive in time for the Christmas sales. I think my mom missed that feeling of accomplishment much more than the loss of pay she had to endure in order to receive seven hundred dollars a month from Social Security.

A year into receiving her government retirement checks, some of the changes in Social Security made by Congress helped my mom reinstate her work hours, but we shouldn't be fooled. These changes were simply manipulating the return of what was hers from the beginning. Though the talking heads on Capitol Hill touted it as real solutions for the elderly, in reality it was just another shameful display of the kind of control politicians have over other people's money.

WAR ON POVERTY

The Culture of Compassion, hand in hand with a willing media, offers many varied descriptions of the poor today; so much so that guilt and pity have become mechanisms for wealth redistribution, and compassion is a political platform upon which to run for office. But do we even know who we are trying to save? Which poor is government to redeem? Are they all the same? The crying lack of a coherent answer to these questions is costing us dearly.

As Robert Rector pointed out in a study for the Heritage Foundation, in 2001 welfare spending in America exceeded $400 billion. That is a whopping 14 percent of the federal budget. That's more than a billion tax dollars per day being spent on various poverty programs, yet Rector's data shows that less than twenty cents of each dollar actually gets into the hands of the people society is trying to help. Social concepts such as "permanent underclass" and "at-risk youth" have become pretexts for entire federal departments with multimillion-dollar budgets. Yet those classified into these categories are still in considerable social chaos. Out-of-wedlock birth rates have escalated to 30 percent nationally, 70 percent among African-Americans, according to the Census Bureau and the U.S. Department of Health and Human Services. Numbers from the National Center for Juvenile Justice show that seven out of ten youths in our criminal justice system come from single-parent households.

Since there is clear evidence that family breakdown contributes to low academic and employment achievement, propensity for crime, drug use, and sexual promiscuity, perhaps we should be asking if the money spent to alleviate poverty has discouraged traditional family formation. If so, does the fact that taxpayer investments in poverty programs have actually hurt the poor justify congressional hearings to investigate at least gross mismanagement, if not outright government corruption or political fraud? There's never an independent counsel around when you need one.

Inside-the-Beltway types have argued about government welfare programs since the Great Society began in the 1960s. Think tanks such as the Heritage Foundation have contended that liberal social engineers created (some say deliberately) an entitlement culture for illegitimacy and poverty to skyrocket. A burgeoning lower class of people dependent on the government will likely continue voting for the party that keeps the handouts coming, and the fundamental motivation of many politicians is to remain in power. Despite growing evidence to the contrary, organizations such as the Center for Urban Policy Research continue to claim that racism, sexism, and capitalism are fundamentally responsible for the problems of the poor, but if true solutions are developed, these organizations could be obsolute. Actually solve those problems and half the liberal campaign platform evaporates. Self-interest will always be the driving force behind the machinery of politics. We need to admit that and move on.

The debate heated up in 1994 when the Republican-controlled Congress aggressively sought to radically change welfare for the first time in history and in 1996 forced former President William Jefferson Clinton to sign their reforms into law. To tone down forty years of contention and offer more opportunities for local communities to get involved in helping the poor, President Bush came to office in 2001, proposing a new "faith-based initiative." But can solutions to poverty really come out of Washington D.C.? What kind of answers will come from encouraging more religious institutions to receive tax-funded government checks for charity work?

Most liberal religious organizations believe federal government should assist the poor through centralization, with no judgment that the poor person is at all to blame for his condition. These groups readily support government coercion over taxpayers to subsidize and run poverty programs. On the flip side, most conservative religious organizations insist on rugged individualism and believe it is the sole responsibility of the poor to change his condition. As such, these groups typically oppose government subsidies and entitlements. How does the federal government control which poor people these faith-based groups are to help, or not help for that matter? How will the religious institution control its mandate to set up parameters for assisting people in need? This path is fraught with hazards once separation of Church and State is considered.

For hundreds of years, religious people have prayed every day that the needy not be forgotten nor the hope of the poor be taken away. This prayer request is in the denominational liturgy of Catholics, Episcopalians, Methodists, and Lutherans. For the followers of Mosaic Law, practicing acts of charity is mandatory, so Jews throughout history have established and supported a plethora of private assistance networks in their communities. There are many signs throughout our society that there is no shortage of desire to help people in need. Even some unconventional religious, faith-based, and secular organizations have set up programs to serve the underprivileged and down-trodden.

Questions still linger, however, regarding what qualifies as need, what type of assistance would really help, and who should pay for it. Our corporate response to poverty has been less than commendable. We cannot even agree on a standard definition of poverty. After forty years of participating in a "War on Poverty," declared by President Lyndon Johnson in his State of the Union address on January 8, 1964, would someone please tell me again what exactly it is we are fighting? And with such an astronomical capital investment, why aren't we winning?

I do not ask this question of politicians because the term poverty has become so subjective and self-serving in most of their minds that it is faceless. Poverty in political terms simply means manipulating tax dollars to keep a variety of federal, state, county, and local bureaucracies functioning and government workers employed. Neither have I asked this question of religious leaders, for their answers must follow the form of their specific programs, at the expense of certain objective criteria. Most private charities are struggling financially for existence or begging for mobilized volunteers, each trying to hold its own beach-head in the war on poverty.

So who will define poverty today?

In order to get a clear picture of what poverty looks like today, we have to discuss three general groups of poor people:

1. the economically challenged,

2. the lazy poor,

3. the poor in spirit.

To be fair, many wealthy people might fit some of the characteristics I will use to describe these three groups; however, to establish some ground rules for this book, I will be focusing on the people in these groups who have little or no money. Once you understand the circumstances, behavioral patterns, and choices of today's poor, you will agree that the battle we face is so complex it cannot be solved with one-size-fits-all government handouts to individuals or to organizations.

If the illustrations herein seem crass, please keep in mind that the examples describe real people in real situations—people who have been assured by sociologists, psychologists, pathologists, and academics that someone else will solve their problems; people convinced that there are political remedies for their dilemma whatever that dilemma might be and that society is going to help them.

I am not one of the learned elite who have simply studied the poor: I am one who has lived the life, overcome it, and still has friends, family, and associates in each group. No one is served by sugarcoating the issue. These situations are real, often desperate, and we must open our eyes to the reality of what poverty has become. The painful truths of these situations show clearly that as long as we allow mere economics and materialism to define poverty, the poor will never be equipped to battle the unseen enemies in their midst.

THE ECONOMICALLY CHALLENGED

Last Christmas Eve, when my older sister Avis got home from working a nine-hour shift in the Wal-Mart jewelry department, she bragged about how her department had sold $22,000 worth of merchandise. "Does she make a commission?" my eleven-year-old Rachel asked, puzzled that her Auntie Avis was so excited with the sales. "No commission," I answered, "but when someone works hard and becomes good at their job, sometimes the reward is a pride of ownership."

How could Avis, who was already working forty hours a week, take on a part-time job that barely paid above the minimum wage and enjoy it? Avis and her husband divorced when their son David was very young. She raised David on her army salary, often working a second job in order to provide for him. After twenty years in the military, Avis retired and settled in South Georgia where David was to attend high school. Her new part-time job at Wal-Mart was to help her son with his upcoming college expenses.

Avis's excitement from those Christmas Eve sales was not about the money she would earn. It was about the hope that came from doing something that could potentially help her son to become a computer technician. The sales energized faith, the substance of things hoped for and the evidence of the things Avis could not yet see.

The economically challenged are the poor that often are invisible to us, yet we are repeatedly in contact with them. They are the bus boy at our favorite restaurant, the gas station attendant, the gardener, the dry cleaner, and the valet. They take our tickets as we enter the theater. They sweep the halls of our office buildings, and they bag our food at the grocery store. Some forget to give us ketchup as we drive through their fast food windows or slam our change on the counter at the local convenience store. Others wash our cars or watch our kids before taking the bus to take care of their own.

I call the people in this poverty group "economically challenged" because, although money isn't everything, a little extra would make such a difference. Any way to save a dollar or gain a dollar is considered. They bargain shop, clip coupons, and recycle newspapers and cans, all the while anxiously waiting for Ed McMahon to knock on their door. They will sometimes buy lottery tickets, gamble in casinos, and study television game shows hoping to one day go on and win. Perhaps because they are the ones most affected by government abuse and manipulation, this poverty group is forever looking to be encouraged. Most of them are faithful to attend church services each week, committed in their love for their family, and hard working.

More often than not, they lack confidence in a competitive

environment and are therefore vulnerable to accepting a lesser position. The education provided by the public schools in their neighborhoods is inferior to those in neighborhoods with an abundance of private schools where the competition for students exists. They receive a lot of rhetoric about government education programs like Head Start. Each election year they are promised improvements to the failing public schools in their neighborhoods. The economically challenged are also the ones most negatively affected when the government involves itself in the affairs of business owners and their employees with legislation like minimum wage. Mandates for a "livable wage" make great sound bites on the evening news, but the reality is that most new laws passed to regulate the business community to protect the economically challenged end up narrowing their opportunities to advance.

The majority of employment and job opportunities in this country are provided by private businesses, not major corporations, as the media often leads us to believe. Many of these private businesses operate on very tight budgets, especially those businesses owned by minorities or located in economically depressed communities.

When the government mandates that these business owners increase wages, the business must raise prices to pay for the increase. Since competition does not allow the business to price itself out of market, it must look at other ways to cut costs, which often means that someone already economically challenged will soon be laid off. This cycle of forcing a business to increase its costs disproportionately hurts the economically challenged. For those who keep their jobs, not only do their soap and toothpaste cost more, canceling out any benefit of a slight wage increase, but also their workload increases because the business now has fewer workers.

The only true beneficiary of minimum wage laws is the government, which collects more sales tax on the higher prices. Higher prices means higher taxes, and the struggling poor cannot understand why although government demanded they get a raise, they have no more money left over than before. It gets worse.

When small businesses are forced to increase prices in order to pay the newly mandated wages, some communities cannot afford to absorb the higher costs. This is often the case in poorer neighborhoods, which accounts for many of the boarded-up storefronts. A decline in sales will force some owners to close the business. Ironically, instead of receiving a government mandated "livable wage," the employees can end up receiving from another government program altogether: the unemployment insurance fund.

Government mandates of all types usually hit the economically challenged hardest. Taxes are the worst. People in this poverty group don't complain much about excessive government because they have more immediate problems and concerns. The simple challenges of life offer such pressing obstacles to overcome that there is precious little time or energy to hold their political representatives accountable.

"Our service truck will arrive between nine and five," says the utility company clerk. Nine to five? Can you be a little more specific? I can't afford to miss a whole day of work to have my phone turned on!

"This is a notice that your rent will increase 25 percent beginning next month." The answer to where the renter is supposed to scrounge up the extra $170 a month was not passed down from the boardroom to the accounting department. In fact, the question never came up.

"Your vehicle registration is about to expire. The renewal fee has increased, and you must come into our office to reapply. Our office hours are 8:00 to 5:00, Monday through Friday and late payments are subject to penalties."

"This letter is to inform you that condom distribution machines have been approved for installation at your daughter's junior high school. Instructions on usage will be part of the new curriculum assigned to all health classes. Parental concerns and questions will be addressed this Wednesday morning at 10 A.M. in the school library—only."

We all have to deal with the various schedules of life, but the economically challenged are significantly burdened. How they survive, and how their dilemma impacts society is a great mystery. Once unraveled, light will be shed on the urgency of limiting the role of government in their lives.

In Chapter Eight, I will attempt to closely examine the latter portion of this vital question. Right now, I want to break this poverty group into two categories to assess how the day-to-day circumstances of life affect the economically challenged. Based on my work with the poor, I have seen that two types of people make up this poverty group: the weary and the hopeful.

The Weary Poor

"What a friend we have in Jesus, all our sins and grief to bear." These are the words to a song sung in many of the fifteen-member storefront inner city and rural churches all across this great country. The song reminds me of the mother of Damian Williams, the young man we saw on national news crushing a brick on the head of Reginald Denny after pulling Denny from his truck during the 1992 L.A. riots. Williams's mother captured my attention during the trial of her son when she reacted to the eight-year prison sentence he received for his crime. Ms. Williams cried out from a courtroom pew and asked the Lord to spare her boy. As the courtroom guards led her son away in handcuffs, she kept calling, "Jesus, Jesus."

I felt sorry enough for this stranger to shed a tear on her behalf. Here was a woman who perhaps worked hard all her life, did what she knew how to do, and now she was watching her son, bound in chains, being escorted away to jail. Hers was a cry of weariness that comes from years of struggle.

Some years ago there was a poster with the caption, "Hang in there." The picture showed a frantic cat with his claws dug in, yet still sliding down the wall. This is a perfect image of the weary poor. They believe they have done all that they can to be successful, yet success always happens to somebody else. Deep down, they think that God plays favorites and likes other people better. The weary poor thrive on the belief that God has blessed everybody who makes it on television or to public office. The celebrity is there to bring them joy in tough times, and if they just hold on, their political leaders will help their plight. They get a great boost when they see an interview with their favorite movie star. That person must be more valuable than they are, so in getting to know the actor a bit more personally, there is a sense of identification: "If I could just get a celebrity's autograph, I would be important in the eyes of my friends and family." The momentary gratification to touch fame vicariously gives them a sense of worth to plead their poverty case to God once again.

It is true that a lot of sin accompanies the weary. They often make bad decisions and then blame their choices on providence. Many have grown weary of trying to succeed. "What difference does it make?" or "I'll never get ahead" are common phrases of the weary poor. While most in this poverty group think life is a game of chance and they simply have bad luck, others, like my friend Emma, think their lot is nothing less than a punishment from God.

I met Emma in 1987, and though we developed a friendship, we lost touch over the years. Then, in the late spring of 1998, Emma called me looking for temporary refuge and needing direction for her life. Because of my travel schedule, I needed help around the house, so Emma came to live with me.

Twenty-five years prior, Emma had come to the United States from Belize hoping to become a seamstress. Although she could sew very well, immediately she began doing domestic work to pay the bills. Over the eleven years I had known Emma, I took every opportunity to encourage her to pursue her dream of becoming a seamstress. I offered to help her, but Emma was often depressed. Her hope to be a seamstress had been deferred for so long that she had given up.

Emma believed she would never get ahead financially or make a garment for someone to buy. She had trouble keeping a car or an apartment. Her English was very broken, and she always had an excuse not to find the time to attend school. She drifted from one low-wage job to another and finally started working the graveyard shift as a security guard for a grocery store.

"God must really be mad at me for all I done," she would tearfully confide. "I try but what's the use. He don't do for me like He do for you."

The roller coaster lifestyle had taken its toll, and her faith in God had worn out. Emma would regularly meet a new boyfriend who seemed to disappear after the sex became too routine for a passing fling. Emma was an avid Bible reader and attended church often, but conviction didn't seem to set in until after the guy would split. Then she would attempt to turn over a new leaf. That was the case when she came to live with me. I don't know how much thought she gave to my offer of help with school and locating work as a seamstress, but by the end of summer Emma had made up with her boyfriend and moved back in with him.

One problem for the weary poor is that they lack the confidence to really believe that they have the ability to make their life better. They don't understand that a small attitude adjustment could open their eyes to big opportunities. Conversely the problems that stem from persistent self-doubt exacerbate their vulnerability to politicians and social experimenters.

The Hopeful Poor

On New Year's Eve of 2000, I was on a missionary trip in Peru. As the founder of an organization geared toward helping the poor, the Coalition for Urban Renewal and Education, I've worked with the poor in many parts of the U.S., but one of CURE's supporters (who I'll call Gene here) suggested I see poverty from the perspective of another country. We arrived at the Iglesia "Remanente De Dios" Church in Iquitos, Peru, that Wednesday evening just as the worship service was beginning. I comfortably hummed a familiar tune, "O Rind the Sky," with a couple hundred Spanish-speaking congregants as they stood for an hour on the cold cement floor singing praises to the Lord.

After the three-hour long Bible study, the pastor of the church ushered me through the crowd to tour the elementary school they had recently started. He was very proud of it and enthusiastically showed off every corner and detailed every great and small feat. The classrooms he bragged about were dreary and bare. I was thinking, *Ninety percent of U.S. prisons are nicer than this!*

For a moment my attention was drawn to the wooden desks resembling weather-beaten picnic tables, then to the cement walls, the cement floor, and the musty damp smell. But what crowded my mind were all the excuses I had heard from dozens of inner city pastors as we at CURE were urging them to open schools. The "every church a school" project we had launched was for more than post-welfare recovery; it was for the restoration of entire communities. Our project saw the churches not only as alternatives to the Department of Social Services but also as restoration centers, not just for souls, but society too. Unfortunately, selling the idea to urban leaders whose Rolexes and Lexuses did not need restoration was more difficult than I had thought.

"We now have 302 students," Pastor Elias Valles Win proudly announced. *In this dump?* my mind responded quietly. *No carpet, no chalk, used books, and limited running water. The ACLU and NAACP could raise millions of fund-raising dollars to shut this school down!* Touring the school actually rejuvenated my zeal to continue pressing the pastors back home. "We are very hopeful for our students. They are learning about God in school and they are very happy." I could not help thinking that "learning about God in school" and "happy" are two phrases no longer used to describe poor students in the United States. No public school student in America ever has to hear about God in class again, but they will surely learn about being gay—which should not be confused with a synonym of happiness.

Happy? No, most of the poor students in the U.S. are trapped in values-free, government-controlled schools and are far from happy. That word came up again as Gene and I toured Belin, the poorest section of Iquitos. The people living in this jungle build their straw-roofed homes like boats, so when the Amazon River floods during the rainy season, they will float.

My escort through Belin was a slender, modestly dressed Peruvian woman named Isabella. She ran the Christian outreach center located on stilts at the corner of an outdoor marketplace. We walked silently together through the open market until sundown. Because she spoke only Spanish and I only English, our communication was mainly through facial expressions that secured a bond of trust. She trusted Gene so she trusted me, and I trusted Gene so I trusted her.

As evening set in, the odor of the marketplace became so foul that I didn't want to walk about any longer. So we climbed the splintered staircase up to the outreach center and sat on the porch waiting for Gene to return from his early evening business appointments. Gene was well known throughout Iquitos because he regularly visited with suitcases full of goodies from the United States. He and his wife, Bridget, financially supported many of the Peruvian outreaches and schools, including the one headed by Isabella. When Gene finally arrived, we loaded our things into his vehicle, and as we drove away, dirty, scantily clad kids swarmed around our car like flies. They were waving, laughing, and playing.

"In one month this entire area will be flooded with seven feet of water," Gene said softly. "Many of these kids following us have just recovered from the snake bites they suffered during last year's storms. The last time my family and I visited here my daughter asked how these kids could be so happy." He shook his head. I would have wondered the same thing except I had already learned to appreciate the happiness that often accompanies many of the hopeful poor.

Materially, the hopeful poor possess very little. It would serve no purpose for Esperian or Equifax to list a credit profile on this group. Most of them would not apply for credit anyway. They use layaway plans for major purchases and go without everything else. This is the poverty group that is almost enviable when it comes to their ability to be content.

The hopeful poor live as if they are blind to million-dollar advertising campaigns and are puzzled by those who would spend $25 thousand on a car or live in a three thousand square foot house. They could not tell you the location of the local mall. (Who is Ralph Lauren, they might ask.) Kmart and Wal-Mart are close enough to designer shopping for this group. They rent movies on video for weekend entertainment, and when they have saved enough money in a cookie jar, a Saturday night splurge at the local Denny's is in order. The people in this category raise their kids in modest apartments without complaint. They often work six rotating days a week and use their tax return to pay for car insurance, hoping that there is enough left over to get all the kids a pair of new shoes at Payless.

The hopeful poor are the ones that reject all handouts but truly love all gifts. "I don't need no charity!" is the response of many in this group when someone is trying to bless them. Sometimes it takes a moment to persuade them that a gift is not the same as a handout, but once they are convinced and receive the gift, prepare to hear "thank you" every time you see them again for the rest of your life.

My friend and former part-time employee, Judy, is a good example of the hopeful poor. Her cheerful disposition has a way of lighting up the room when she enters. You would never guess from her million-dollar smile that life has been hard for her financially.

Judy's mother died when she was very young, so she was raised by her grandmother in North Carolina and spent her teenage years with her aunt in California. She took her strict religious upbringing seriously during high school and married her first sweetheart while still a virgin.

The newlyweds both worked hard enough during the first year of their marriage to put a down payment on a quaint condominium. Two years into their marriage, Judy got pregnant. Three years into their marriage, her husband lost his job. Six months later, the bank foreclosed on the condo and the auto lender repossessed their car. Judy and her husband have alternated working odd jobs and odd hours for fifteen years, and their family still struggles to pay rent, grocery shop, have bus fare, and keep the lights on in their apartment. Their limited skills kept them from stable or well paying jobs while their limitless love gave them another daughter and room in their home for the infant son of a wayward nephew serving jail time. As low-wage workers it is difficult to juggle their work schedules so that one of them can be home with the children. But Judy still has that million-dollar smile, and her family would never know that the government has classified them as poor.

It is a shame the economically challenged are the ones centralized government misleads the most. The hopeful have such optimism about life that they have great trust in their elected officials. The weary have such pessimism about life that they have no one else to trust. Both categories actually think their political leaders are looking out for their best interests, and they would cover their ears if someone tried to convince them otherwise. The economically challenged really believe the reason their children's public education is substandard is because the schools need more money. The reason their streets are full of potholes and trash is because the city needs more money. The reason their neighborhoods are unsafe is because of poverty. Consumer prices are high because of capitalism. Property taxes are high because of institutional racism. They believe these things because their political leaders told them these things, and they absolutely know that their leaders would not lie about something so serious.

What keeps the economically challenged deluded is their misguided trust. Most of them put too much confidence in the word of their elected officials. So strong is this trust, they hand over their children for the government to educate, their freedom in exchange for government-mandated rent control, and large portions of their wages so the government can provide for them in retirement. So sincere is this trust, they do very little personal planning for their future. In fact, according to information compiled from the Population Reference Bureau and AmeriStat, approximately 80 percent of the people in this poverty group have Social Security as their only means of retirement income. Eighty percent do not have life or health insurance. Ninety-three percent do not have a savings account. And 95 percent do not have a will. I wonder what percentage of the economically challenged have asked themselves what happens if the government fails to deliver on any of its political promises?

THE LAZY POOR

"Let me make sure that I understand you correctly," I inquired of the welfare caseworker as I presented her with my pregnancy confirmation note from a doctor. "All I have to do for you to send me $465 a month, $176 worth of food stamps, and 100 percent free medical and dental assistance is keep this baby. As long as I don't have a bank account, find a job, or get married I qualify for aid? Where do I sign up?"

For me to hear those rules to go on welfare—or what in 1980 we called "the county"—was like winning the lottery. Ever since I was arrested for shoplifting and narrowly escaped arrest for committing armed robbery as a teenager, I had been looking for a legal way to finance my laziness. Now at twenty-three, I had finally found a source of income that did not require work.

Being the middle child with an older sister and brother and a younger sister and brother, I had grown up accustomed to delegating all work, including my household chores. I would steal money from my mother's purse and pay my siblings to do the work I couldn't muscle or whine my way out of doing. I did not want to work for anything, so I would steal property and money from neighbors or local merchants. I lusted after the finest of designer labels and desired a lavish leisure lifestyle, but I was lazy. I simply refused to work hard. I blamed racism, my parents, and any other excuse society would allow me to use for my laziness. My attitude of victimization, coupled with my unwillingness to develop the habits necessary to attain financial independence, led me further into poverty. My desires quickly turned into resentment, and my lusts escalated into the covetousness that led me to sign up for welfare that day.

The lazy poor is the one poverty group for which a central government must facilitate welfare services through guilt and manipulation of the rest of the populace. This social pressure against the diligent and law-abiding is rooted in America's alleged responsibility regarding its treatment of blacks during and after slavery, which we will look at in more detail in Chapter Three.

Taxpayers generally despise this poverty group, because regardless of how expensive the welfare programs are, the lazy poor always want more. This poverty group loves pleasure, wine, and oil but always demands that others improve their lot when welfare services prove to be substandard or fall short. They seldom give thought to working hard for pleasure. In fact, they depend on the pity of liberal politicians to redistribute wealth, so they can get what they want with little effort and no personal responsibility.

Unlike the economically challenged, whose tax payments basically offset most of the government benefits they might receive, the unique social consequences, social reactions, and social costs caused by the actions of the lazy poor are a financial drain on our entire tax system. These actions of the lazy poor create stimulating headlines, turn up the volume on policy debates, and thrust entire communities into deplorable conditions. I will break down the lazy poor into three different categories, each with a similar mindset or attitude, but distinct behavior. The categories are:

1. the careless,

2. the sluggard,

3. the scoffer.

What I hope you will come to understand as I explain the behavioral patterns consistent within each of these categories, and how they work uniquely in concert with the other categories of this poverty group, is that these very patterns are what have created new ground rules for the war on poverty that we are dealing with today.

The Careless

Early after my Christian conversion, I was so unclear about my obligation concerning the poor that, while I volunteered to help widows and orphans, I would look at street beggars with utter disdain. I was so ashamed of most of the things I had done to end up on welfare that I thought surely the vagabond was not the poor and needy worthy of my defense. Every time one of those shopping-cart-pushing, dirty bums would ask me for spare change, I angrily told him to get a job.

This went on for about a year, until the day I saw one of my old, drug-addicted boyfriends sleeping on a bus bench with all of what was left of his belongings in a box under his head and a shopping cart to his side. The Lord then touched my heart and whispered to me: "There but for My grace . . ."

I immediately thought of the two years I shacked up with this guy, living a life of parties and drugs. Smoking crack cocaine had led him to the mental state that landed him on that bus bench. The night freebasing was introduced to our household, I declined because I was too sick and uncomfortable to "party" having just had my fourth abortion. That night was only the beginning, but my fading interest in him kept me away from his new drugs. During the next few months, things grew intense. I found another bed partner, became pregnant again, and moved out having never smoked crack.

As you will see when I detail my story in Chapter Two, I was able to get my act together and take a different path than that of my ex and was able to temper my attitude with compassion. Still, the question surrounding the poverty of my ex-boyfriend involves his attitude. Should taxpayers help my ex-boyfriend because his drug addiction has left him poor? His problems were self-inflicted. He was careless. By now he could be dead.

The reason that most of the careless poor have problems is that they live a whirlwind life. Often, they are too lazy to make responsible choices because any thought of tomorrow is a distraction from the fun they are having today. "I couldn't care less," are words that not only describe their attitude, but their lifestyle as well. The careless are reckless and sloppy. The careless poor stay poor because they don't really care that they're poor. They care less about their families, their friends, their jobs, and their things than they do about having fun. Personal injury and bankruptcy lawyers love the careless poor. They run up their credit cards and then file bankruptcy. They will litigate against their boss, their neighbor, or their own insurance company for the smallest misunderstanding. These poor don't care if they curse in front of children or their parents. Their homes are filthy, and they do not mind. They also don't care about killing the baby in their womb or abandoning their offspring. Many in this poverty category not only live recklessly, they also spread poverty to others.

"Girl, there are two nine-year-olds and an eight-year-old here," my oldest daughter's friend, Angie, reported over the telephone from her biological father's house. Bert, as I will call him, invited all of his children to visit for the holidays. In nineteen years, I don't think Angie had seen him nine times. He had five children from five different women, only one of whom was ever his wife. At the time that wedding took place, the bride was carrying his baby, and another woman was pregnant with another of his children. The marriage lasted all of eight months. Three of the women who gave birth to children fathered by him spent time on welfare, including Angie's mom. Three of the women have other children. None of these women are currently married. He is still making babies.

What public program or social service could help alleviate the poverty of this complex situation? Sex education has been taught in the public schools of the careless for twenty-five years. Access to free condoms? They don't care to use them. Access to free birth-control pills? They don't care to take them. "Go for it," is their motto, "what do I have to lose?"

Some social experts would argue that the source of this type of poverty is economic and cultural. They believe if society would invest more money into the construction of midnight basketball courts and new job training programs, we could change the environment that leads to such reckless actions. These government social workers believe bad behavior is due to some external force.

How far do they take this belief? They say that the two million people in prison today simply need rehabilitation. They say the biggest problem for the three million women on welfare is child-care. The estimated 150,000 people with HIV need access to health care. Drunkards are victims of a disease. Gluttons are victims of a weight imbalance. Looters are victims of racism. And sexual predators are victims of, well, human nature. The careless poor are prime targets for government program experimentation by the social engineers of the Great Society. Every negative act of mankind's fallen nature has a specific federal department to fix it or a special research grant to help cushion the consequences.

When the question of personal responsibility arises, vehement opposition arises because of the connotation of sin. The political elite governing social programs will not allow religion to interject even the concept of sin into public discourse regarding the abuses by the careless poor. A mere discussion of eternal accountability renders the social expert powerless and perhaps in need of a new line of work. The tragedy is that when government safety nets replace natural consequences, the careless poor are effectively chained to the sin that will keep them in poverty.

Intolerance toward religious input is so out of control that to call someone in this category a sinner could actually land you the role of defendant in a lawsuit. I know you think I have to be exaggerating, but when the Congress was in debate over President Bush's faith-based initiative in the summer of 2001, the only way it survived the scrutiny of the secular Left was to make it illegal for the faith-based grantees to proselytize. Imagine you are running a local job-training program funded by a grant from the government and you tell a welfare recipient that God could help them. For doing what faith-based organizations have always done and what they do best, suddenly your program could be shut down.

If you did talk about moral accountability to one of the careless poor, I don't think you have to worry much about litigation. Unless the careless could get some money for punitive damages from a lawsuit, their response to your suggestion would probably be the rolling of their eyes or the shrugging of their shoulders. Remember that "fools mock at making amends for sin" and most of the people in this category respond to everything with either "whatever" or "who cares."

The next category of the lazy poor might actually prefer it if your job-training program were shut down.

The Sluggard

If you visit any one of the government housing projects across this country, you will see one of the biggest differences between the sluggard and the careless: work. Generally speaking, the careless will work (which is why they so often get away with their destructive behavior) and the sluggard won't (which is why taxpayers subsidize every area of their lives).

The main reason the sluggard bathes in welfare programs is welfare by its very nature is a system that encourages this type of laziness. It is free! You are given housing, food, cash, healthcare, childcare, and bus fare. What more could one need? The only thing that the sluggard has to do to receive these wonderful benefits is to go apply for them. Now for most in this poverty category that is an effort within itself: to get up out of bed, put on some clothes, and go to the welfare office. "Why can't we apply over the telephone?" they might complain. In fact, complaining competes with watching television as their favorite pastime. The sluggard complains about having to take the bus to the welfare office, the grocery store, or the doctor even though the bus tokens are free. They would prefer to inconvenience a friend to drive them.

The complaints and excuses of the sluggard are so consistent they could be the lyrics of an old blues song. About finding employment, the song begins, "No cab fare. No new clothes to wear." The catchy tune reaches the media pundits, and they add a verse or two to this song of the sluggard. "Kids are starving. Old folks freezing. What can these helpless people do?" Then an entire liberal choir adds a chorus, "Capitalism, capitalism, dirty, greedy, mean. Wealthy people, white people, they're the ones to blame. Republicanism, conservatism, racist, sexist, misers. We the people, caring people, the sluggard we defend!"

This category of the poor has skyrocketed out-of-wedlock birth rates nationwide, pushed AIDS rates toward epidemic proportions, and mounted illiteracy rates to where 50 percent of today's youth cannot read the condom packages others demand on their behalf. They have children without even the thought of marriage because sexual responsibility requires discipline, and the sluggard has no discipline. They then complain about the quantity of the handouts they receive. "What am I supposed to do with this?" they ask sarcastically, suggesting that the portion is not sufficient to meet their standards.

This category of the lazy poor is helped most by time limits and work requirements in welfare reform. They won't leave home without them. How long will you slumber in front of the television, O sluggard? When will you rise and turn off Jerry Springer? They lust after designer things but will not learn how to design for themselves. They lust after having a car but will not learn how to drive. One way to ensure that the sluggard never gets on the path toward financial independence is to continue distributing welfare. God made winter for a reason.

Some politicians believe they are doing the sluggard a favor by addicting them to a government-subsidized life. They believe that if we would just offer more personalized and localized services these poor, helpless people would not need to venture so far away from home. Of course, the buildings that will administer these new programs will boast the name of the legislator who twisted arms to get it so the sluggard will always remember and vote for his friend.

In looking for alternative ways to motivate people to leave welfare, the White House Office of Faith-based Initiatives is suggesting marriage incentives. While this might be an attractive gimmick for the careless poor, it is not for the sluggard. Marriage is work, and to get the sluggard to work, someone will have to make them. The problem with trying to convince the sluggard that they should marry is that if the relationship turns abusive they will require more intervention services. More often than not, the sluggard's attitude toward marriage is "no one is going to tell me what to do," i.e., "a spouse will nag me about lying on the couch all day, complaining on the telephone, or watching television." No sir, they would rather get their goods from the government, and if the government tries to tell them what to do, they can simply go sing their sad rhythm and blues song to the scoffers.

The Scoffer

The scoffer threatens the masses to either finance government social programs or else watch America's inner cities burn down. Arrogant and proud are the best adjectives to describe them. They claim welfare benefits as "entitlement" and are assured by vile politicians and misguided civil rights leaders that their voices will be heard in Washington D.C.

When I consulted with the Heritage Foundation and the GOP Congress in 1994 on welfare reform, the reactions of the scoffers were of great concern to me. The 1992 Los Angeles riots were fresh on my mind because I was still trying to recover from the aftermath. Every aspect of my life was shaken during those three days of massive burning, looting, and murder. The small business I had built over eight years was totally destroyed. I was publishing a local Christian events guide and most of my advertisers' offices burned down.

"There goes my income," I thought as I drove past the burning businesses in an attempt to get my children and myself to our home safely that first night. "Home, what home?" My apartment building was still intact, but most of my neighborhood's stores were in flames. National Guard tanks parked at my grocery store, and merchants were on the roof of the corner ice cream store with rifles. It all started because three white police officers were acquitted for viciously beating a black motorist—an admittedly large black motorist hopped up on PCP—for resisting arrest. Although there was some justification for anger and frustration after the verdict, I knew that much of the rioting embodied the entitlement attitude and that scoffers were in charge.

While my public persona was growing, I accepted every opportunity to tell my story of leaving welfare. I viewed sharing my testimony on network and national television, as well as in national newspapers and magazines, as witnessing for God. It would not be long before the scoffers began to confront me. My story is one they do not want made public because it exposes the weakness of their trump card, known to most as the race card. If too many blacks start talking positively about free enterprise and independence from government programs, scoffers lose the ability to sit around on their self-important rear ends and blame others that the cushion is not soft enough. Remember, we are talking about the aggressive segment of the lazy poor.

Immediately, the scoffers sent hate mail calling me a "sellout" and "Uncle Tom," but I remained confident. I continued to tell my story of deliverance from welfare dependency to any and every audience willing to listen. Soon the names became curses, and the offenses got more ugly. Police escorts became necessary when lecturing on several college campuses. By the time I started hosting my own radio talk show, the scoffing had escalated to death threats against my children. The story I tell reveals the truth the scoffers want silenced. The lazy poor cannot get rich. Unfortunately, the attitude of the careless, the excuses of the sluggard, and the arrogance of the scoffer will keep them forever impoverished and demanding that government officials fuel, or at least *feel*, their pain.

THE POOR IN SPIRIT

Oh that this was the only group the war on poverty was waged to defend, for they are truly in need. Life dealt them a raw hand and has beaten them badly. Bruised by family and wounded by strangers, they are vulnerable; they are fragile; they have been stepped over, stepped on; and now they are shattered. There is only one category in this poverty group, and it is called broken.

The Broken

"Humpty Dumpty sat on a wall. Humpty Dumpty had a great fall." What? None of the king's men could come up with the perfect piece of legislation to pass both the House and the Senate, be signed into law by the president, be declared constitutional by the Supreme Court, and be guaranteed to put Humpty back together again? What discouraging news for those who were broken before they even had the opportunity to get up on the wall in the first place.

Today, broken people are scattered everywhere. Sixty percent of American kids are growing up in households with no father. The Department of Health and Human Services (HHS) reports that approximately 2.8 million children are abused each year. According to a survey conducted by the U.S. Department of Justice in 1994, 2.5 million of the nation's 107 million females twelve years old and older were raped, robbed, or assaulted in a typical year, or were the victim of a threat or an attempt to commit such a crime.

Each of the individual stories behind these statistics is so compelling that American taxpayers spend $80 billion annually on mental health care, and an additional $6 billion is spent on mental health research. Our criminal justice system is plagued with psychiatric testimony. Some six million American children are taking prescribed mind-altering drugs such as Ritalin. Other fellow Americans simply give up and commit suicide every year. In fact, in the interval from 1979 to 1996 there were a total of 535,890 deaths in the U.S.A. that were reported to have been suicides. According to the U.S. Surgeon General, suicide is the eighth leading cause of death in the United States, claiming about 30,000 lives in 1997, compared with fewer than 19,000 homicides. When tragedy strikes, it doesn't discriminate. People in this poverty group cross all financial, racial, and religious spectrums.

Government programs cannot help the broken poor because their poverty is in their heart and spirit. There are no political answers because their questions are deep and moral. One-size-fits-all approaches are ineffective because, although the common denominator of the broken is pain, their pain is unique, individual, and very personal. So there is no scientific or technical solution. There is no faith-based government initiative that can help because the primary tool of government is force. Only charity is volunteered, and true charity is what they need.

When people in this poverty group are in pain, access to all of the medical insurance in the world cannot heal them. The drug-addicted vagabond can have her babies delivered at the finest of hospitals thanks to Medicaid. Yet why doesn't she avail herself with free prenatal care or other medical benefits except via the emergency room? Perhaps her sunken condition is the result of living life as a runaway after having been the victim of domestic violence and incest. A centralized, secular government may insist that in order to help this broken woman it needs to build more tax-funded clinics in her neighborhood, but how would this address the source of her poverty? Shame and despair have enslaved her to self-destruction. Her poverty is internal, and political socialism cannot adequately address conditions of the heart. That is the work of religion.

Unfortunately, our lawmakers and courts have banned religion as a weapon in its war on poverty, thereby leaving the poor in spirit to live a roller coaster life of chance. Even the great faith-based initiative makes it illegal to emphasize the essence of any particular religious belief.

I wonder if the reason most Americans settle for the type of war on poverty being waged today, with no clear definition or common goal, is that we don't want to think about it. The poor make us uncomfortable—the unpardonable social sin. So, we will condemn them to the hell of mediocrity and debasement, and pay handsomely for the privilege, as long as it keeps them out of our sight. Only they won't go away. They will never go away. And it is time for our government to realize its war on poverty is lost, indeed was lost before it started because a committee could never solve it. The problem is too multifaceted, complex, and personal for machinelike bureaucracies to fix it. Decades of expensive, failed policies should send a message to our legislators that, verily, their cheese hangeth out in the wind. The lower class is not a mere political pawn for arrogant experimentation. The one-size-fits-all social solutions are doomed from birth because the slate of problems varies greatly from person to person. More government will never be the right answer. We the people must come together, face the ugly realities of the social climate of America with honesty and common sense, and gradually peel the reigns of control over poverty from the hands of government and divisive political organizations. We must work to create new possibilities for those who still can be helped, one person at a time.

2

Learning the Hard Way:
My Story

"What are you doing living on welfare?" the pastor asked emphatically. Sitting among four thousand other churchgoers that Sunday morning, you would think I could have hidden from the insistent voice posing this question. It was 1983, and I had received welfare checks from Aid to Families with Dependent Children on the first and fifteenth of every month for more than three years. There was no hiding from the pastor's question. I knew he was talking to me.

I was first exposed to the ease of collecting welfare in 1976 when I moved to California from New Jersey. Living recklessly in the fast lane and dismissing all authority, I was experiencing many of the consequences, including several venereal diseases and multiple pregnancies. The government must have had a hotline into the darkest and most dreadful places I journeyed. Provision was made to ensure it would not be necessary for me to take responsibility for my actions and lifestyle. Every time I contracted a sexually transmitted disease, I was sent to a "free" clinic, which would give me medicine. Medicaid was there to pay for an abortion to end my pregnancies. General relief was available with a welfare check for every bout of unemployment.

"The government is not your source!" the pastor continued. What does he mean the government is not my source? Government welfare was my source—my only source. I believed I was entitled to receive government welfare anytime I wanted it and viewed it as an unlimited resource. This belief was intrinsic to my worldview. I didn't realize my belief system had trapped me in spiritual and economic poverty. What else could I believe considering my life experience?

A ROCKY BEGINNING

By the time I was twelve years old, I was bitter, rebellious, and violent. I began to make reprehensible behavior choices that only seemed to mount as each birthday passed. At fourteen, I was committing vandalism. By sixteen it was assault, battery, and petty theft. After being arrested for shoplifting, only to receive high-fives and other accolades from my friends, I escalated quickly to burglary. Seventeen brought a high school life filled with classes and track practice during the day, but at night an acquaintance and I would break into houses and steal money and property just for kicks. It was not long before I allowed myself to be talked into armed robbery of a liquor store. That was the final straw. I knew this was a horrible crime for which I could end up dead or in prison.

Wanting a fresh start, I moved to California, but without the Lord I was at the mercy of my own undisciplined ability to self-govern. When I reached L.A. I made behavioral changes, all right; I replaced fighting with drug abuse and stealing with sexual promiscuity. By nineteen I qualified for not only champion standing as part of the lazy poor but also first runner-up in the careless category.

My days typically began at noon, just in time to watch my soap operas. Afterwards, I would thumb a ride, smoke pot, and roller-skate half-nude at Venice Beach until evening. Then I would dance at the local disco until last call, before leaving with some strange man. For income I would work odd jobs, take a couple of classes at the city college to get free grant money, or get pregnant and collect a few welfare checks, then have an abortion a couple of months later.

After my fourth abortion I began to notice my life was completely out of control. The third abortion had been the first eye opener. I went to a new clinic because I had used different names and Medicaid stickers at the clinic where my first two abortions were performed. The receptionist there seemed to have recognized me the second time, and since that was only three months prior to this new pregnancy, I decided to use a different clinic.

I was uneasy when the doctor came into the room to perform the abortion. Not because this was my third abortion, but because he was white. Without saying a word he started the procedure. "Hey! What happened to the anesthesia that puts me to sleep?" I said. "We don't do that here," he responded coldly. It was the same cold inflection I heard earlier when the receptionist greeted me.

The other clinic I had frequented was in the ghetto of South Central Los Angeles, but it was clean, had plush carpeting, soft couches in the lounge, pretty pictures on the wall, and piped in classical music. This new clinic was located near Beverly Hills. The walls were stark white, the chairs hard, the tile on the floor cold, the receptionist grumpy, and the doctor was mean. I wanted to be put to sleep so I wouldn't have to think about what was happening. "Stop moving around" he said, while prodding with his surgical instrument. "That hurts!" I shouted. "You'd better shut up and be still or I will stop what I am doing," he callously snapped back. I helplessly left that clinic feeling vulnerable, empty, and wondering, "What exactly was he doing?" My thoughts were quickly interrupted as I boarded the crowded bus on Wilshire Boulevard and found a seat. As the bus headed in the direction of my home, I began to think about the drugs waiting for me there. Get home, get high, and forget. My anxiety left.

Shortly after that experience, I moved in with a new boyfriend, the one who eventually ended up sleeping on bus benches. As usual, there was no discussion of marriage. Having bought into the feminist message that equated marriage to prostitution and slavery, I was as hostile to the concept as he was noncommittal. He seemed like a cool guy at the time, but my standard of measurement was pretty low. I reasoned that at least when he impregnated me I would not have to go to the abortion clinic alone. I thought that this had to be a good thing because he took me to the Westmoreland Clinic, which was considered upscale and of top quality. He even told me of some celebrities who went there for their abortions.

Our free love attitude had cost the taxpayers another abortion fee, but this time I had a feeling in my gut there had to be something wrong with continuously killing my babies while they were still in the womb. Even though my friends, television, radio, print media, and certain very vocal circles of our society conveyed a message contrary to what my conscience was telling me, I left the clinic this time vowing I would never abort a child again.

During the "wait a few days before you have sex again" period, when life was supposed to return to normal, I started to hate my live-in boyfriend. My reckless behavior intensified, and not a day would pass that I did not get high on drugs. Within a few months I was pregnant again, and this time it was not my boyfriend's baby. Knowing his temperament and drug disposition, my boyfriend might have killed me if he found out I had been messing around on him. My first thought was I had to move, and fast. The only place I knew where an unemployed, drug-addicted, pregnant runaway rebel could go for help was the government. I could think of no other option but the Department of Social Services. Besides, they had worked hard in the past to save me from the natural consequences of my actions.

CAUGHT IN A TRAP

"LarStella Irby!" The clerk yelled over screaming babies, snoring drunks, pregnant teenagers, and other welfare applicants. "Take this number, and when you hear it called, go to that door." "Will I get a check today?" I asked, grabbing the number she had slapped onto the counter. "I need to move!" My number came up just as my favorite soap opera ended. I smiled and thought this must be a sign. LarStella was my birth name, after my Aunt Laura and Aunt Stella. A residual of the era of slavery when children could be sold off never to be found again, it was common for blacks from the South to mix names of relatives just in case. It wasn't until a cute Italian man I met in my late teens told me Stella meant star that I took on the nickname.

As my caseworker reviewed my paperwork, I commented about the zodiac symbol displayed on her desk. It was supposed to be compatible to mine. She was about my age, twenty-three, and her disposition let on that we had more in common than it appeared. "Look," she whispered over the desk. "If you want to get along with me, do not open a bank account and do not get married." "Cool," I responded, "but I need to move. Will you give me an apartment voucher for a place to live?"

Previous experiences with welfare while seeking abortions and other assistance had schooled me on exactly what she was after. She did not want to spend her time seeing me. She instructed me on how to fill out the monthly CA-7 form to ensure that I would receive my checks without having to come back to her office. She sent me away with food stamps, free health care, and a voucher for a deposit on my new apartment. Her job required that she visit and perform a home inspection for each voucher she issued, but a few days later, she called and canceled the scheduled home inspection. "I'm going to lunch with my girlfriends," she announced, "so if anyone asks, just pretend I came by." "No problem," I responded. Just like that I was hooked. Welfare became my source of sustenance, and I became dependent on the government.

Now this pastor was challenging my economic worldview, after almost four years of bellying up to the government trough. "God is your source, not the government!" As the Sunday morning message continued, those words began to cut away at my old mindset. Like a thirsty wanderer happening onto a fresh brook, I flipped through the Bible that had been given to me three years earlier by Ken and Gerald, two inner city businessmen who had introduced me to the Lord. They ran an advertising agency in the heart of the Crenshaw District of Los Angeles. I met them one day when I was looking to supplement my welfare check with some "under the table" cash in exchange for clerical services. Ken and Gerald said they did not pay under the table because it was illegal. I had to laugh. Mainstream life was so foreign to me, and the thought of these two good-looking brothers trying to respect "the system" seemed ludicrous. Did they not know that this is a white man's world designed to keep blacks from getting ahead? I mocked them for implying my lifestyle was unacceptable. Unacceptable? To whom?

Every influence in my life told me I was in charge of my own destiny. "Life is chance, and values are relative. I can do whatever I think is right" was the survival philosophy I learned from my public schools, the music on my stereo, and the programs on my television.

The events of the past several years reveal the natural consequences of a society embracing that philosophy. People blowing up federal buildings, mailing letter bombs or anthrax, disposing of live newborns in dumpsters—these are all acts that seemed right to those who carried them out. This type of moral relativism, taken to its logical extreme, can even justify using airplanes as human bombs to murder innocent civilians. I found it easy to reject the concept of faith because all absolutes were judgmental, but I had not thought my philosophy through to its inevitable end. I could shun the idea of family because it was sexist, and the concept of community is worthless if you only look out for number one. Besides, I was convinced America was racist, and if I didn't get them, they would get me.

Understanding I had bought into the lie, Ken provoked me. "You can do anything you want to do, and you can believe anything you want to believe." Ken then looked me in the eye, put his finger in my face, and told me my lifestyle was unacceptable—to God. God? Who was he kidding?

The next time I saw Ken was months later. I had been taken to the hospital to have labor induced so I would prematurely deliver my baby. In addition to my drug addiction taking its toll, I had preeclampsia, a condition characterized by high blood pressure, swelling, and in my case, toxemia. Fortunately, all of the toxins cleared as soon as my daughter was born, but her low birth weight left her in critical condition and both of us in the hospital. During the entire two weeks we were in the hospital, Ken was my only visitor.

LEAVING WELFARE

Now, more than three years and a hundred Bible studies later, I was hearing the same message that motivated Ken and Gerald to refuse my services. Before the pastor could finish his sermon, my heart was stirring with the desire to find real purpose and meaning for my life. For the first time I felt a sense of personal responsibility for the choices I had made and would make. At twenty-six years old, I was beginning to accept the fact that I had an obligation to at least try to take care of my daughter and myself without assistance from the government.

It was not an easy decision I was facing. I had believed the message in black America that whites hated us and would not hire us. It was entrenched and magnified every time a leader or representative that wore my skin color spoke. I had very few personal experiences with whites, so I couldn't be positive I would be able to get the type of job

I would need to support my child. Whites owned the real jobs, and it was hard to imagine they would ever give me one. Much of my limited work experience was for small and struggling black businesses that could rarely meet payroll.

I had worked at the air force base where my dad was stationed the summer before my sixteenth birthday and was raped by a military captain. After that I shifted in and out of a few waitress jobs and even spent some time in the circulation department at the *Los Angeles Times*. As I considered cutting the umbilical cord to the government, I couldn't help thinking that if those customers and coworkers were reflective of what to expect in the real world beyond welfare, forget it!

My parents had sheltered us from the racial tensions mounting in the civil rights movement, even though the year I was born was the year Rosa Parks made her big stand by keeping her bus seat. My dad was stationed in Moses Lake, Washington, then. Televisions were rare in 1956, so news traveled a bit more slowly. Growing up I saw a lot of white people, but life on that military base and every other station over the next ten years was segregated. We did not eat in their restaurants nor stay at their hotels. When traveling across the country to get to our next base, we either slept in the car or displaced friends and relatives from their beds at 3:00 A.M. My parents never explained their actions; we just did what we were asked and kept our big mouths shut.

The year Dr. Martin Luther King Jr. died we were stationed in Japan, so my dad could more easily assist with bringing the wounded out of Vietnam. I played with a lot of Japanese kids, but whites and blacks did not mix. In retrospect, Dr. King's death was one of those "Where were you?" moments. Yet when my brothers, sisters, and I heard our parents crying for the very first time and asked what was the matter, our response upon hearing the tragic news was "Who?"

Returning to the States a year later to scorched cities and insidious racial hatred from both sides, I gravitated to the militant blacks. I was twelve and looking for a reason to rebel. We lived in East St. Louis,

Illinois, a short distance from the infamous St. Louis court where the *Dred Scott* decision was handed down stating that blacks were less than human.

Less than human. From what I was hearing about how slaves were treated and now—one hundred and four years after emancipation—how fellow blacks were still being treated, I made up my mind to show white people that "less than human" could apply to people on both sides of the conflict. Of course, hatred and bitterness never solve anything. Bigotry is bigotry no matter the color of your skin. No amount of suffering, past or present, gives you the right to be a racist, regardless of your political affiliation. By the time my dad got new transfer orders, however, I had already embarked on my secret life of street crime and drug use.

Attending an integrated high school in New Jersey with a 99 percent white faculty only served to fuel my suspicions and fears. There wasn't much trouble between the white and black students there because we only mixed in class, and then only because most of the seating charts were alphabetical. In the mid-seventies, every black still knew where the lines were drawn and which lines you dared not cross. Although the South continues to get a bad media rap about its racist past, the racist attitudes in the North, while a bit more silent, were no less evident. These attitudes played out in every community I experienced, every school I attended, and every job I worked.

Add to that the sad fact that my favorite line of work to date had been selling stolen goods collected with my night-life friends. And that pastor with his just-say-no-to-welfare message couldn't help pushing me nose to nose with a personal crisis. Seven years in and out of collecting government checks had done nothing to prepare me for the world of honest work now set before me. Stepping out would require a deep-rooted trust to turn over my finite well-being to the caring hands of an infinite God.

I left that church determined I would finally learn to live free.

CHANGING MY WORLD VIEW

The next day I wrote a letter to my caseworker and told her to take my name off of the government dole. Three months later I was still unemployed and completely broke. I was behind on the rent, and my friends were getting tired of feeding me. Finally, an opportunity opened up. I heard about an entry-level, temporary job answering telephones for a food distribution company. This was a low-wage, part-time position that paid less than welfare and offered no employee benefits. I am sure that more than a few liberals would look down on my decision to take this job. They believe work of this nature is meaningless, worthless, and demeaning. But I didn't care that it offered less than their perception of a livable wage; it was my fresh start.

What I needed was the opportunity to prove to an employer and to myself that I could be trusted to not steal from the business, stick it with a lawsuit, take drugs on my bathroom break, call in sick, or waste company time gossiping. My new worldview would require discipline and self-governing, something I knew had been painfully absent from my life. I needed to develop the integrity to not slip back into any of the habits that left me unemployed and on welfare in the first place. Setting personal career goals enabled me to look to the future and believe there would be something better beyond the low-wage, part-time, void-of-benefits, uninspiring employment I had taken upon leaving welfare.

If I had listened to any of the brain-dead, paternalistic jargon coming from the elite legal minds stalking about the halls of Congress with their hands out, I might have assumed that not only was this job beneath me but also leaving welfare was a desperately foolish thing to do. My ears were getting smarter, though; at last I had learned enough to not fall prey to that woefully misguided line of thinking. Not once did I view answering those telephones to take condiment orders from restaurants as a waste of time, or worse, an irrevocable step into the always-at-risk population of the working poor. I knew I had to start somewhere, and I had no intentions of staying at that level indefinitely.

My dream was to transition from that entry-level position into owning my own business. What I needed from that particular job was income to cover rent, food, clothing, utilities, and childcare. I chose to contribute to that employer consistency, diligence, and a merry heart. In return, I began to develop some of the skills necessary for fulfilling my dream of business ownership. Seeking business ownership as a goal helped me understand the difference between what was urgent and what was important. It was not urgent that I earn fifteen bucks an hour or have a company retirement plan. Childcare was not an immediate concern because setting goals had taught me the disciplines of sacrifice and compromise. I was able to keep childcare costs low by sharing an apartment with two roommates who also had children and work schedules that allowed us to juggle babysitting responsibilities.

When I appeared on the *Oprah Winfrey Show* in 1996 to defend the congressional changes proposed in welfare reform, I was confronted with hostility as I challenged the supposition that the women to be affected by the reforms would be condemned to menial jobs. The opposing team, five welfare defenders and Oprah, argued that unless Congress increased the minimum wage, provided childcare, healthcare, education, and full employment to create the tax base to pay for it, welfare reform would cause poor children to go hungry and homeless. "An entry level job is not the end," I shouted in order to get a full sentence heard. "Dream bigger than minimum wage and government handouts," I told them. I really wanted to share my personal experiences with them, but the format was designed for their agenda, not discovering the truth. All I wanted to do was convince the women on welfare that they too could be successful without depending on the government, but my ideas were discarded with anger and resentment.

It took me by surprise that even Oprah did not defend my position. During the show I became quite frustrated because it seemed I could not draw a clear enough picture for her to support the reforms. How do I explain to the queen of television talk, the epitome of rags-to-riches herself, that the answer to poverty is freedom and personal responsibility—not the welfare state! Desperately I tried to challenge the one lady on the panel who was still on welfare, repeating the very pitch I had made to thousands of poor women all around the world. In housing projects, homeless shelters, halfway houses, and maternity homes, my message was overwhelmingly welcomed. Facts did not appear to matter, however, as she became more adamant by the minute that she would die and her kids would starve if we changed the rules governing welfare benefits.

I could relate to the fear that she was experiencing. Being asked to get a job when you have severe impediments is not easy. Fear is one of the biggest hurdles to overcome, and it was obvious that was the real challenge for her and the other welfare moms in the audience. My first fear after leaving welfare was that I would not be hired even at an entry level. I was taking some business courses at a local college, but since my prior proficiencies were in drug abuse and stealing, it was an uphill battle. It's often said you never get a second chance to make a first impression. I had a silver cap with an engraved star on my front tooth, knew little of the corporate ethic, and did not have a reportable or credible work history.

An even larger obstacle was my belief that white people were racist and would only hire blacks when forced. It might sound foolish, but in my mind it was true. The very few blacks I knew who worked for whites had government jobs in public service, public education, or in the military. The fact that Ken and Gerald owned their own advertising business was the only example that gave me hope and allowed me to put my fear aside as I entered that first job.

Every time I answered the telephone for that food distribution company, I acted as if it was my own customer and the client on the other end was worth a million dollars to my business. The encouragement I tried to share on Oprah's show was a confidence that hard work would open new opportunities to leave welfare and poverty forever.

OVERCOMING OBSTACLES

This is not to say that my first post-welfare job was a dream job free of any difficulties. The telephones I was assigned to answer were in the orders department located in the sterile basement of a large office building. Salesmen from across the county would call in refills and orders of condiments and other supplies for hundreds of small and large restaurants. I would have to capture their orders handwritten on paper and send it to the shipping department. The more orders they called in, the more money each salesman made, so they talked fast and were rushed, especially on Mondays and Thursdays.

The workers in the shipping department who received the orders were a different story. They were union laborers who received the same wage regardless of whether their delivery truck was half empty or overloaded. The more orders they received, the more they used their backs. So they talked slow and were sarcastic, especially on Mondays and Thursdays. Each rotating shift in the orders department consisted of about twenty people, and the only other black in the department was a thirty-two-year-old female who had been there fifteen years.

On my first day at work she was eager to give me the entire scoop, including how to get away with the least amount of work for the maximum financial benefit—by paying $260 to join the labor union. Every day she would say I was "uppity" because I worked fast and enjoyed it. She complained about benefits they weren't getting and how the union was going to strike and I would have to join.

I knew nothing about unions, but as an ex-street hustler and con artist it sounded like paying for protection. Thinking that $260 ought to buy me a whole lot more then some obscure job security, I asked suspiciously, "What does the $260 get me?" "Benefits," she exclaimed and proceeded to list several items I found no interest in obtaining. "I won't be here long enough to need your union," I explained. "I'm going to start my own business as soon as I finish writing my business plan." My new coworker did not take too kindly to my brash decline of union benefits. Her resentment toward me was immediately evident but grew worse as I continued to fulfill my duties with excellence. Demonstrating a standard of excellence caused other union workers to express their dislike for me too, but I was determined to stay focused on my goals.

One day, the telephones were exceptionally busy, and the salesmen were very impatient. Many of the restaurants were even calling in their own orders. I responded by making each feel they were the most important call I had received all day. As I finished one order my supervisor walked over to my desk and commented, "You sure do talk a lot, and you're good at it too!" I smiled because this was not the first time I had heard that comment. There had been many occasions on which I was told that I talked too much. It was a talent that got me tossed out of school classrooms and on one occasion allowed me to worm my way out of a jail sentence.

To my surprise, my supervisor asked me, "Have you ever considered sales and marketing?" He proceeded to tell me about a full-time position in the marketing department that paid much more than my current wage. It also provided benefits without requiring me to join a union. The job offer gave me a warm sense of accomplishment, but I declined the transfer to the marketing department. My heart was set on completing my college degree and owning my own business.

A short time later the union convinced its members in my department to go out on strike. Rather than endure the risks involved in crossing their picket line, I knew it was time for me to try my hand as an entrepreneur.

FINDING MY WAY

I began publishing a monthly magazine that compiled a calendar of events from various churches around Los Angeles. It also contained editorials that addressed inner city needs. The primary focus, however, was to spotlight wholesome entertainment for single Christians. The first edition consisted of sixteen black and white pages of crooked lines, unedited copy, and advertisements from ten local businesses. The final publication eight years later was sixty-four full-color pages of professional layout, quality content, and eighty advertisements from both local and national businesses. The cover had been graced with renowned entertainers such as Shirley Caesar, Rosey Grier, CeCe Winans, and Helen Baylor.

Things were exciting that first year of launching my business. Advertising sales were slow but consistent. It was hard work to sell enough ads to cover the printing costs, my personal overhead, and the needs of my daughter. My entrepreneurial dream had come true, but good financial stewardship was a challenge. Instant credit and lenient bankruptcy laws made it easy to become undisciplined financially. This is where many people get off the track toward financial independence, and I was no exception. The first time I received the ubiquitous "congratulations, you have qualified" letter from a credit card company, I remember thinking it was a symbol of accomplishment and prestige. Credit companies would send the card without a completed application; all that was required was a signature—your first use was your acceptance of the terms. I began charging business expenditures, food, gas, and clothes. I would lay down gold, silver, or platinum at my convenience. I had ten credit cards, which lulled me into a false belief that I no longer had to work quite so hard selling advertising.

Six years after starting my business, I filed bankruptcy. One year later California went into a severe recession, and advertising sales hit an all-time low. I had to downsize my staff. Two years later, the 1992

Los Angeles riots wiped out what was left of my advertising revenues, as many of my advertisers' businesses were burned to the ground. I had to close my business. My seven-year, already rocky marriage could not sustain the blow and gradually disintegrated over the next five years. I was grief-stricken, but my determination never wavered.

I refused to go back on welfare. There was no way I would look backward or listen to the leftist lies that sought to discourage me from even trying. Every time those seductive deceptions tried to tickle my ears, I would remember depositing more money in a week through my business than welfare gave me in a year. The experience I acquired selling advertising for my magazine made it possible for me to transition from the ruins of my business into co-hosting a talk show on a small Christian radio station in Long Beach.

I suppose I could have reported the station to the wage police because the position did not pay a minimum wage. It offered no healthcare or childcare benefits. In fact, any money I made would be through commissions based on the revenue received from the advertisers that supported the show. There were no guarantees I would be successful, but once again hard work and a positive attitude paid off. Before long I was offered the opportunity to host my own three-hour daily radio talk show with an ABC affiliate based in San Francisco. Not only did they pay a good salary, but they also put a studio at my home in southern California.

CONFRONTING BLACK ANGER

I learned two very important lessons from my radio experience. First, it taught me that if anyone would work diligently and enthusiastically, new opportunities would arise and more income would follow. Second, I learned the essence of a popular quote from Dr. Martin Luther King Jr. "Most people are thermometers that record or register the temperature of majority opinion, not thermostats that transform and regulate the temperature of society."

Talk radio works best when driven by a host who is not afraid to lay ideas on the table that stand out sharply from the prevailing opinion. I was one such host, refusing to support the political ideas of certain leaders just because they were black. Our inner cities were a mess; our schools were broken; our moral institutions were falling apart. Government was becoming more intrusive, excessive, and expensive, and all they could say was "racism!" Their assertions were ridiculous and unsupportable, and I said so repeatedly on my radio show.

Little did I know I was walking into a mine field controlled by the forces of political correctness that would explode against anyone who tried to change majority opinion. After thirty years of social engineering, blacks had become political pawns of the Left, and the unforgivable sin was trying to leave Uncle Sam's plantation. The thermometers of the status quo were very vocal in their disapproval that I was a thermostat.

Leftist leaders had blamed every social ill on racism. Through a coordinated program of distortion and misinformation, they had conditioned far too many blacks to depend on the federal government for solutions, and most of my African-American callers liked it that way. Every show became a shouting match. After a year and a half of hosting my nine-to-midnight show in San Francisco, I transferred to an ABC affiliate in Los Angeles. It was a career move that was supposed to be a step up. My new hours were from noon to three, which was great for my kids and more money for me. I lasted in my new home market just over three months.

As I shared my views on the air, black rage erupted in my direction, starting with vitriolic insults and quickly escalating to death threats. I wasn't surprised, really. I expected to make enemies, and the balance was that I also had many black allies in Los Angeles who agreed wholeheartedly with my position. Thousands in the church community respected me from my magazine publishing days and wanted to hear my opinions, despite their controversial nature. They knew something had gone terribly wrong for us as a community of people, but somehow no one could quite put their finger on it. My views were welcomed as a fresh perspective in a difficult debate.

The hardest part was the yelling, name-calling, and slamming of the phone. Truthfully, it wasn't very good talk radio, and when too many callers came unglued, my boss would scold me for not controlling the show. Despite all my personal progress, I still had a well-honed rebellious streak that ended up in control most of the time. This translated into a default mode where I would out-scream my outrageous callers. Every day after the three-hour shouting match, I'd get called into the hot seat in my boss's office.

Within a month of being on L.A. radio, the homosexual activist community had joined my black enemies. Their first displeasure was my debate with a prominent inner city pastor who was passing out condoms in his church. He was a high-profile supporter of their political agenda, and my popularity within the black evangelical community posed a great threat.

One common tactic of the homosexual activists is to piggyback their issues on civil rights legislation. Honest exposure of the specific differences between marches on Selma and protecting sodomy could pose a serious threat to their movement. Their point of attack escalated the volatility of my show beyond shouting and threats; they went after the advertisers. The station responded by assigning a liberal feminist as the producer of my show and giving her control over topic selection. That lasted all of one month. Some of the topics she chose were "How to Pamper Your Man" and "Ten Ways to Sooth Away Stress as a Working Mother." Not that I totally despise the Oprah approach to living, but frankly, regarding the first subject, I was on the brink of a divorce, and regarding the latter, I preferred that moms stay at home with their children.

One day, when she finally decided that battling me was worse than reading the front page of the newspaper, she assigned me to talk about a Mexican teachers' strike. It was the same day that Benjamin Netanyahu won the elections as prime minister of Israel. As a strong supporter of Israel as an independent and sovereign state, I was elated by the news and chose to talk about it with my listeners. That day I was fired for insubordination.

Professionally, it never looks good for a radio talk show host to simply disappear from the airwaves because it opens doors for idle gossip and celebrity rumors that can be damaging later on. Throughout my radio days I lectured at various colleges, and one rumor, that I was fired because I was homophobic, spread all the way to Atlanta, nearly denying me a chance to speak at Emory University. The Young America's Foundation had to fight for more than a year to get me rescheduled, and even then, when I did speak, the homosexual activist population on campus was livid. My hotel had to be changed three times for security purposes.

Personally, the hardest part of leaving radio was the broken relationship with my loyal listeners. They were my chatting buddies, my friends. In San Francisco, I was their "queen of the night." In Los Angeles, I was their "breath of fresh air." I still miss the intellectual ground we covered together, but if ever being fired from a job was a blessing in disguise, this was it for me. My professional plate was full, and doing a daily radio show often got in the way. I was conducting goal-setting workshops in housing projects, sponsoring policy forums for inner city clergy, and consulting on the federal welfare bill. My lopsided debate on the *Oprah Winfrey Show* happened within a matter of months from the date I was fired. That same year, I also spoke at the Republican National Convention, hosted and co-produced a documentary on welfare reform for the BBC in London, and finished my first book.

I made no attempt to return to radio because my schedule was overloaded. I had longed to work full time with an organization founded in 1995, the Coalition on Urban Renewal and Education (CURE). The black anger and liberal rage that confronted me on radio and at lectures had encouraged me to develop a national think tank for studying and promoting alternative solutions to the social pathologies associated with poverty.

I grew increasingly amazed at the depth of closed-mindedness in my African-American brethren when exposed to new approaches to help mitigate the scourge of poverty. Their perceptions were so twisted by liberal deception that—in the minds of the more extreme in the bunch—because I did not buy into their philosophy and would publicly disagree, I was no longer black. Their hard-nosed hostility against any possible changes in the social policies of the 1960s was unreasoning. Fact and undeniable truth didn't influence their worldview. From the inside, I had never realized what a stiff-necked and obstinate people we were. They demanded to keep welfare, education, affirmative action, health care, and Social Security in the hands of the federal government regardless of alarming failure rates. Any discussion of statistical facts was impossible. They insisted that the unwillingness of whites to let politicians redistribute wealth was the reason the programs weren't working. The time-honored liberal tactic of restating a lie over and over until it became widely accepted had robbed these sad people of their ability to perceive truth, even when it was staring them in the face.

During one heated debate on school choice, a powerful and nationally influential minister I knew and respected told me bluntly, "Anything rich white Republicans are for, I am against." When I asked him what if the idea was actually good for fellow blacks, he said that the person proposing the idea would have to pass his litmus test, which was "Where were you when I was in Montgomery?" This kind of mule-headed arrogance, bitterly flaunting blind presumption in the face of common sense and reason, keeps black people enslaved to their dependence on the government. Men and women like this minister and his willing accomplices in the liberal establishment are involved in the slave trade, as surely as if they had put the chains on the people themselves. We work the ghettos instead of the fields, dutifully putting "massa" back in the Senate or House of Representatives, so they'll keep those compassionate benefits coming. They get power; we get a free ride. Everybody wins. Except we don't. The results have been disastrous.

I know the social problems afflicting black America are great. I know that confronting black anger is exhausting. But I also know the dreams of my ancestors did not include enslavement on the government's plantation of poverty. They understood that nothing in the world is greater than freedom, and I know from personal experience that freedom will never come from dependence on the welfare state.

Welfare is a sociological monster, perhaps birthed with the best of intentions, but now unwieldy and insidious, damaging the very people it was intended to help. If we are ever to slay the beast, we must understand its origins and where it went so terribly wrong.

3

Liberals Hijack History

In early 2003 Nissan Corporation ran an advertising campaign in cele-bration of Black History Month. But some didn't celebrate the automaker's billboards. According to *Auto Week* magazine, Nissan quickly came under attack by activists, including Rev. Jesse Jackson. The reason was that the ads showed the words "black history" with "history" crossed out and "future" written in. Critics claimed that the billboards showed disrespect toward black history. Ironically, the ad campaign was the first major project by Nissan's new minority advertising firm, True Agency of New York.

Rainbow/PUSH, an organization founded by Jackson, was offended by Nissan's strategy because, according to director Glenda Gill, "Replacing history with future sometimes can rest in the philosophy of those opposing the leveling of the playing field for African-Americans." The complainers dismiss True Agency as a "pawn for Nissan's head agency, TBWA/Chiat/Day." Rainbow/PUSH said that the billboard cam-paign would have been preferable if it had said, "Black History is our past and our future."

Is there really a black in America today who doesn't want a future that is very different from the past? Isn't a better future the point of all the civil rights legislation of the past half-century? Nissan Corporation and True Agency should have been commended for the thoughtful and optimistic message they conveyed to the black community. It is the exact message the black community needs to hear because it is true. In our land of freedom, a beautiful future is available for anyone who is ready to work for it, regardless of what they have had to contend with in the past.

I part company with Rainbow/PUSH in our respective ideas about why we learn history. They will claim that the point of learning history is to gain self-esteem. I believe self-esteem comes from taking personal responsibility and achieving. Learning history is part of our responsibility, but we learn it so that we can move on to a new and better future. Movement defines history. The point of the ad was to remember and to move on. It is ironic that psychologists and social workers have their hands full trying to help their patients shake the shackles of their past and the feeling that they are helpless victims who cannot play a role in their own future. Why do the political types view these same pathologies as positive? Or was this just another attempt to shakedown corporate America? Dr. Martin Luther King's "dream" was of a better future. The "promised land" he saw from the mountaintop was a better world for people of all colors and races. Thanks to the liberals hijacking America's past, we are moving in the opposite direction from that dream.

BIG BROTHER PUTS ON WEIGHT

The Great Depression marked a turning point in the American conscience. Until that point, family life was most often governed by the personal faith and traditions of the man of the house. A man's ethics were connected to his religion, and his career often was identified and developed through working in the family business. He used his skill and labored to provide for his wife and children. When he died, the family business was passed down to his heir without a government tax. More often than not, the oldest son took up and continued the traditions, work, and patterns of the father. The hope of the poor rested on their faith in God and their confidence that the American dream could pull them through and keep them moving toward the goal.

When disasters hit, the community pulled together, family helping family and neighbor helping neighbor. Little thought was given to the intervention of federal government in the personal lives of family members. In fact, most Americans were hostile to any heavy outside intervention. The only families for whom this American way of life didn't work were black families. While the American ideal of freedom and opportunity attracted immigrants from around the world who saw the fruit of their labor prosper as they progressed in work and education, most blacks were dragged to America in chains and enslaved. For them the American dream quickly became a nightmare.

At the end of the Civil War, more than four million slaves were emancipated. One million immediately left the South to find work and pursue the new opportunities their freedom allowed only to be met with great hostility and danger in the North and as they progressed west. At the turn of the twentieth century, Americans of all persuasions were leaving small communities and centralizing around manufacturing and mining jobs in big cities. Far from kin and life-long family relationships, when financial hardships mounted there seemed to be no place to turn except towards fear, cultural clashes, and government intervention.

These fermenting social problems came to a head with the arrival of the Great Depression. Beginning in the United States in 1929 when the stock values hit the basement floor with a crash, many people had their finances wiped out almost overnight. Businesses, factories, and even banks closed their doors, leaving millions of people out of work without a dime to their names. Fear spread like wildfire as people realized they could lose everything. This fear led directly to a dramatic change in the national attitude regarding the role of government in manipulating the markets, regulating businesses, and bailing families out of trouble. Over the years, record numbers of Americans grew more willing to pay the variety of taxes demanded in exchange for federal protection and the perception of security in the shadow of the "dark side" of capitalism.

No longer was community and commerce viewed as the backbone of financial stability. Far too many Americans had moved away from the stability found in family-owned and operated businesses only to discover economic volatility. In a surprisingly short time, the masses abandoned 150 years of independence and began looking to centralized federal government for employment guarantees, charity programs, and safety nets. This shift in attitude affected all communities of Americans, including blacks.

Late in the 1960s, a man who had lived through the Great Depression was asked to comment on the feelings of fellow blacks about Roosevelt in those years. His answer can be found in the 1992 book, *The African American Experience*: "Oh yeah, that was something. He broke the tradition. My father told me: 'Republicans are the ship. All else is the sea.' Frederick Douglas said that. Negroes didn't go for Roosevelt much in '32. But the Works Progress Administration came along and Roosevelt came to be a god." In 1932, more than two-thirds of African-Americans voted against Roosevelt. When the election in 1936 took place, 75 percent voted for him.

"Once when Jacob was cooking some stew, Esau came in from the open country, famished. He said to Jacob, 'Quick, let me have some of that red stew! I'm famished!' (That was why he was also called Edom.) Jacob replied, 'First sell me your birthright.' 'Look, I am about to die,' Esau said. 'What good is the birthright to me?' But Jacob said, 'Swear to me first.' So he swore an oath to him, selling his birthright to Jacob. Then Jacob gave Esau some bread and some lentil stew. He ate and drank, and then got up and left. So Esau despised his birthright." (Genesis 25:29-34)

This discourse between Jacob and Esau accurately describes the cultural shifts that took place during the Great Depression. Read that passage again replacing the word "Jacob" with "Uncle Sam," "Esau" with "the People," and the word "birthright" with "freedom," and you will find a vivid picture of how American attitudes changed regarding sacrifice and suffering.

The roles of government, religion, and family were being redefined, and the environment was ripe for change. The needy could now be referred to the federal government.

Toward the end of the Great Depression, corrosive indolence warped a once healthy work ethic, and new cultural ideals began taking a firm hold of society. Once the needy got a taste for government handouts, the genie was out of the bottle. Life, liberty, and the pursuit of happiness became twisted into a perceived governmental obligation to provide happiness to everyone. As the natural cycle of dependence begat a lower echelon of faithful voters, legislators became increasingly willing to let them believe that the alleviation of poverty was the sole responsibility of politicians.

BLACK AND BLUE

The dark side of capitalism revealed during the Great Depression was not the only force driving the paradigm shift in American thought about the role of government regarding the needy. Compassion for others is the first casualty of a people struggling to survive, and compassion for those not like us evaporates even faster. Racial hatred and terrorism against blacks grew and spread quickly, especially in the South. These poisonous historical currents laid the foundation for today's accusations of racism that seem to dominate most political discussions on remedies for the poor, especially in the areas of healthcare, education, business development, welfare, Social Security, and affirmative action.

During the era of slavery, blacks did not hold any social status that posed an economic threat to white achievement or employment. Entering the 1870s, many white Americans resented the newly won freedom and citizenship of black Americans. Whites often used local authorities to force the advancement of white interests as a way of dealing with the competition of blacks in the marketplace. Their methods were ruthless, often brutal. According to *World Book Encyclopedia*, 230 blacks were lynched throughout the United States in 1892 alone. The federal government contributed to, and enabled, the racism by denying blacks the opportunity to transition into the full citizenship guaranteed to them under the 14th Amendment of the U.S. Constitution. In 1883, the Supreme Court ruled that congressional acts *to prevent* racial discrimination by private individuals were unconstitutional.

In 1896, the infamous *Plessy v. Ferguson* Supreme Court decision upheld a Louisiana law requiring "separate but equal" accommodations for blacks and whites in railroad cars. Southern states used the "separate but equal" rule established in that case to segregate the races in public schools, transportation, recreation, hotels, and restaurants. Northern states barred black migration and participation through labor unions and trade associations, particularly in housing.

Tensions continued to escalate, and by 1920 the white supremacist Ku Klux Klan boasted more than two million members throughout the country. Founded in Pulaski, Tennessee, in 1866 by former Confederate soldiers and sympathizers to oppose radical reconstruction policies and protect white supremacy, the KKK enjoyed renewed legitimacy in business and religious circles in the early twentieth century.

Amidst rising unemployment, limited food supplies, and public pressure in the 1930s, the established religious community, again most notably in the South, saw a resurgence of participation in racist activity and substantial support for forced segregation. Ignoring the horrors of the KKK's campaign of terror—including whippings and lynchings— "White Only" signs sprang up at public and church facilities, and what was worse, many KKK nightriders were upstanding members in the Church.

One might expect that a civilized country would soon rally around an oppressed and maligned people, especially within its own borders, but turning a blind eye was commonplace. Between the years 1882 and 1968, according to *World Book*, some 3,445 blacks were lynched in America. That is equivalent to about one lynching every eight days and doesn't include blacks who were simply murdered by more conventional means.

Participation in vile and aggressive racism by established religion created a new dilemma for America. Historically, the religious community had always taken the lead role in caring for society. Established religion had been a sanctuary for runaway slaves and the bedrock of protection and assistance. In fact, it was the religious community that since the Revolution had appealed to Congress on behalf of freedom for the slaves. In addition to building hospitals, universities, and colleges, religious organizations provided charity services for the needy regardless of their heritage. That was where we found our orphanages, food kitchens, temporary shelters, and employment referrals. Whenever someone was in despair, regardless of his or her race, church and religious societies were the first place to seek help.

Something changed dramatically in the motivation of these religious groups after the stock market crashed. The sons of former slave owners began to wait in the same soup and shelter lines as the sons of former slaves. Expressions of racism, both moderate and extreme, loomed throughout society, quickly overshadowing Christian love. Many white religious orders and denominations developed codes, rules, and policies against blacks. Some Christian publications, universities, and theological scholars cited the Negro as inferior, while other Christian associations barred black memberships. Popular religion in America, former refuge of the downtrodden, put on blinders and refused to recognize that beyond the segregation signs, the life created for blacks was a blight against the very Judeo-Christian ethic upon which our nation was founded.

After international news broadcasted the 1956 acquittal of the murderers of Emmett Till, the fourteen-year-old Chicagoan who was brutalized, tortured, and drowned in Money, Mississippi, in August 1955 for allegedly whistling at a white woman, the federal government could no longer ignore the crimes against humanity committed under the watch and with the blessing of certain local civil authorities and religious orders. Demonstrations resulting from the death of Till helped Rosa Parks light the flame for the civil rights movement that ensued. The battle between state and federal governments that followed forced religious leaders to choose between constitutional mandates for inalienable rights and the right of the states for local governance. Conservative religious organizations sided predominantly with states rights. That decision was the turning point that cost religion its integrity and credibility with regards to the care for the needy. Ultimately, it would cost the religious community its authority to answer the hard questions of civil justice that need moral interpretation, leaving the arena of compassionate care for the needy and abused in the greedy hands of an impersonal government machine.

RIGHTING CIVIL WRONGS

The victory of World War II left Americans in a strong economic position. "Happy days are here again" was a sort of national anthem in 1945. Black military men, however, returned to the status quo of discrimination, racial terror, and financial hardship. Poor black families, who at that time in history represented the largest percentage of Americans living in dire poverty, were at the top of every political discussion regarding the expansion of New Deal social programs.

The hardships of poverty and the threat of egregious racism in South Carolina is what prompted my dad to join the Air Force in 1949. He was the oldest of six boys my Grandma Warreno was raising alone and felt a special burden to contribute financially to help lighten her load. He had heard that the military was offering educational and economic opportunities that simply were not available to young black men in his hometown. Although the sting of racial prejudice was still present inside the military, it was controlled to the degree that all of the men in the service had equal opportunity to employment and education. My dad was no exception. He completed his high school degree and worked and traveled worldwide as a cook for the next twenty years.

African-Americans endured ninety years of cruelty and horrific racial hostility after slavery ended and the movement for civil rights began. Some families were untouched by it only because they lived so far in the country that neighbors were dependent on each other's well-being regardless of their race. My mom's family knew everybody around them in the country hills of Traveler's Rest, outside of Greenville, South Carolina. White and black neighbors worked the fields together, ate together, played together, and fed each other when times got tough. Mom said she had plenty of white friends in her neighborhood as a child, and the only time she was reminded of "her place" in society was once a year when they'd go to town to buy a pair of new shoes for Easter. My granddad was well respected and known for generously sharing the produce from his hundreds of farmland acres.

He protected his wife and large family against the night cries that they would sometimes hear in their woods behind their house by staying alert and maintaining healthy relationships with his church and his neighbors. Mom said she always knew when a lynching had occurred nearby. On those ghastly nights, she would hear lots of cars and then some laughter, and then the cars would slowly drive away. The next day she knew not to ask her daddy if she could go down the street to play.

Where were the organized religious bodies when twenty-five million fellow Americans were being harshly treated and scorned because of their skin color? Unfortunately, during the entire civil rights movement, the religious community in America missed countless opportunities to invoke the God-given moral authority needed to make a difference. With their eyes and ears closed to the racist atrocities being perpetrated, sometimes just down the street, many white congregations sat safely on the sidelines, leaving the black congregations to become the pillars of the movement demanding moral justice and marching for equality. Facing battering water hoses, brutal beatings, half-cocked shotguns, and vicious police dogs, blacks abandoned all hope of finding an ally in organized religion and instead found new partners for their movement: American Jews and liberal scholars.

The first made sense. The latter was a big mistake.

Jews gravitated towards the civil rights movement because of their historical experiences living through the Diaspora, always under pressure from hostile governments and prejudiced peoples. As survivors of the still-recent Holocaust, many Jews were motivated by a natural sympathy for the plight of American blacks while others were involved because they had a vested interest in making sure that America held onto her constitutional mandates and allegiance to provide liberty and justice for all. Even the Jews who felt no sympathy knew instinctively from long centuries of oppression that if victimizers of blacks went unopposed, persecution of the Jews would not be far behind. Individual Jews rallied behind the movement with financial resources, media connections, and personal commitments of time and energy. They knew how to use the legislative and court systems to open opportunities for justice and worked with the black civil rights leadership to raise public awareness and influence political action.

Relationships between Jews and blacks thrived at the beginning of their common cause. When Dr. King was in charge with his message that "you cannot legislate morality but you can regulate behaviors," it was easy for them to lock arms with him and face the potential of jail or death together. When the focus of black activists became increasingly political, however, Jews felt compelled to distance themselves from the movement. As a community of people, Jews on the whole did not look to the government to solve their social and economic problems. Their overarching desire was simply to be left alone. They would take care of their own problems and build their own businesses so long as the government maintained civil order to protect their interests.

After the death of Dr. King, the civil rights movement changed the focus of its efforts from removing the barriers of segregation to forcing integration. The traditional civil rights groups apparently forgot that Dr. King had said while government "can keep a man from lynching, it cannot make a man love." By the end of the '60s blacks had become immersed in politics, demanding that their quest for true equality would include legislation that forced integration, such as mandatory school busing and affirmative action programs, a journey most of its Jewish followers refused to take. This parting of the ways laid the foundation for the environment for much of the black animosity toward Jews we see today. That Rev. Jesse Jackson, a once-respected champion of civil rights, would stoop to call the city of New York "Hymietown" in 1984 to a *Washington Post* reporter demonstrates just how far relations between Jews and blacks had deteriorated by that point.

For the last thirty years of the twentieth century, while blacks spun their wheels trying to search out political redress for racism, only to watch their communities and families fall apart, the Jews embraced capitalism and watched their businesses soar and prosper, leading to thriving family and community life and opening major doors of influence both socially and politically. In 1965, black businesses heavily patronized by local residents were the economic backbone of their neighborhoods. But, according to the U.S. Bureau of Labor Statistics, by 1995, after decades of misguided political "remedies" enacted against discrimination, 65 percent of working middle class blacks were employed by

the government, and 30 percent worked for corporations that were subjected to EEOC or affirmative action guidelines, leaving a once growing
black business community as barely a footnote in history.

Throughout the civil rights movement and up until 1965, Census
Bureau statistics show that 78 percent of black households were com-
prised of intact families with a husband, wife, and children. But by 1995,
after the political manipulations of the welfare state, black marriage
rates had dramatically declined, and 69 percent of its children were
being birthed outside of wedlock. Left to wonder how two outcast communities of people could start in a similar place of dislocation and end
up at two radically different destinations, blacks began to feel that Jews
owed them something since they were major consumers of the products manufactured, produced, and sold by Jews. Jews, on the other
hand, after working hard and making major sacrifices to develop their
businesses, felt no such obligation. These feelings of resentment and
self-pity continued to receive regular massages by tension-instigators
such as Maxine Waters, Jesse Jackson, Louis Farrakhan, and Al Sharpton
and, over the past ten years, have erupted into open distrust and anger
between Jews and blacks.

HISTORY AS HOSTAGE

Rev. Jackson raised a stink when, in his easily-provoked estimation,
Nissan devalued black history. It's peculiar, however, that he hasn't
raised even a peep over the outright theft of our history by liberal academics and radical socialists who've used *our* plight to agitate for *their*
causes.

Prior to the civil rights movement, liberal scholars and black leaders debated over the supposition of America's founding fathers that a
Creator endowed human rights upon mankind. The black clergy used
this premise to support their desire for equal rights, while liberal schol-

ars challenged the very concept of creation as antiquated and irrelevant. In fact, many academic professionals, social scientists, and eugenicists based their research on the notion that blacks were naturally inferior to whites due to an incomplete evolutionary experience. This type of reasoning led to earlier horrific social experiments such as the Tuskegee project to inject syphilis into imprisoned blacks and Margaret Sanger's Negro project to control the population of blacks through birth control and abortion.

By the 1960s, things had changed. An entirely different sort of weed was burning on campuses across America, and the hope of Dr. King started going up in smoke as the civil rights movement began breaking apart into vying factions. The influence of Malcolm X's "by any means necessary" incited hostilities that, upon his death in 1965, spurred race riots in some major cities in the North. The Black Panthers emerged soon after and were perceived by moderates as threatening the momentum that had been gained by the traditional civil rights groups. Still, black berets sported by Bobby Seale and Huey Newton were catching on as stylish and culturally hip. Black power symbols and Afros were overshadowing the posh and polished black clergy who had marched with Dr. King. His was a movement of the soul; theirs was a movement of the fist, and the gangsta style of the Panthers attracted the disaffected youth of black America who had no desire to join the mainstream. His was a movement to get education; theirs was a movement to get even. He wanted revival; they wanted revenge.

Black leaders gave up trying to sort through the despair that followed the assassination of Dr. King in 1968 and the ensuing race riots and began calling upon the liberal academic community to help them steer civil rights issues toward more governmental education and economic remedies as the movement transitioned into the seventies. Liberal scholars and social engineers gladly took the helm as a way to expand their experimental society. Much had been accomplished at the theoretical level, but the plight of the black community offered them live subjects on whom to test those theories.

Academics had long supported the idea of centralized government, as long as a properly educated liberal elite would be in charge. Now they had a way to get what they wanted.

As they do today, liberals in the press and universities (institutions in which they continue to predominate) used class warfare to manipulate the issue of poverty for their own political gain. All it took was focusing the lens of history on past injustices to the exclusion of almost anything else. Most of the modern liberal thinking about race and poverty is rooted in an attempt to atone for racial injustices against black people on American soil. The politics of guilt and pity were used to blame slavery on all Americans who were not black and then convince these same Americans that redemption rested in providing poverty programs. The tortured reasoning of the Left maintains that wealthy people are, and have always been, the reason black people are downtrodden and poor.

After the civil rights movement confronted the government, the segregationist laws were torn down, and those formerly oppressed by segregation became classified by the government as a victim group needing special protections and special treatment. Certainly some protections and special treatment were warranted at the outset, in light of the harsh methods of the white supremacists and segregationists, but with the immediate threat past, the ongoing characterization of blacks as victims became just another way to keep the lower class in its place.

It is hard to imagine that liberals foresaw the full effect their policies would have on black self-esteem, but they were quick to capitalize on it in their campaign policies and rhetoric. The theme of class warfare became a powerful weapon in the arsenal of the Democratic party. If there was a problem in the black community, finding a way to blame it convincingly on rich white people was guaranteed to win votes.

The real losers in the process were the blacks themselves, and, to a lesser extent, the American people. Blacks suffered plummeting self-esteem and hopelessness—prevented from focusing on future achievements and directed to dwell on past defeats—while the rest of the populace was made to feel somehow responsible for causing the whole situation. By politicizing an issue that should have remained in the arena of morality—of right and wrong—the issue became less about how to solve the problem and more about how to make one political party look better than the other.

"Compartmentalized Brain Syndrome," a tongue-in-cheek term coined by Balint Vazonyi, is a malady that has infected the gray matter of numerous American political and social leaders and is quite contagious, affecting millions of Americans. Now, to catch this rampant fever that seems to be growing at a phenomenal rate, especially on college campuses, conditions must be just right: a fundamental weakening of logic, a reliance primarily on emotion, and a strange acquiescence to accepting responsibility for someone else's actions. Add to that a vague sense that we have it better here in America than anywhere else in the world, and the conditioned mind is ripe to accept the guilt of a nation—for slavery, for war, for the suffering of the Native Americans. In the hands of liberals, history becomes an indictment. Without a religious context, the only way we know how to assuage our guilt is to pay for it. Show me a rich person awash with the guilt of our nation, and I'll show you a liberal politician nearby with his hand out.

Liberals drew African-Americans into their philosophy to gather the poor onto Uncle Sam's plantation—easy to do when a demoralized people were told their only hope was the State.

ON THE PLANTATION

Social engineers of the late 1960s told Americans that black people could not take control over the poverty in their lives due to centuries of

racism and segregation. These social scholars and government special-
ists convinced the masses that poverty was a societal problem, one the
government must fix.

President Lyndon B. Johnson declared, "We have the opportunity
to move not only toward the rich society and the powerful society, but
upward to the Great Society. . . . This administration today, here and
now, declares unconditional war on poverty in America. . . . It will not
be a short or easy struggle, no single weapon or strategy will suffice,
but we shall not rest until that war is won." President Johnson worked
with his Democratic majority in Congress to establish the Department
of Housing and Urban Development (HUD), as well as the
Department of Transportation and Medicare. Johnson pushed the Civil
Rights Act of 1968, saying it would end racial discrimination. The term
"Great Society" caught on, and since that time has been used to
describe many of Johnson's domestic programs and those that would
follow. These programs included the expansion of government welfare services, public education, providing for the elderly, and aiding
urban areas.

Most of the blame for poverty and racial disharmony was placed at
the feet of the wealthy and the white. Equal opportunity became a big
issue because of the uncivilized tactics used to keep blacks from voting
and gaining employment. The Great Society agenda concluded that in
order to level the playing field for the needy, the masses must consent
to government-mandated wage increases, rent controls, and forced integration. White Americans could only atone for the sins of slavery and
segregation through support of poverty programs and by redistribution
of their wealth through taxes. Black Americans were told greed was the
reason wealthy whites prospered and that these wealthy whites were to
blame for economic barriers that stopped blacks from obtaining success.
Anyone who disagreed was labeled a bigot.

Working Americans were being intentionally trained to feel guilty
for the victims of poverty. Simultaneously, the poor were being taught

that their poverty was not their fault. The poor were convinced that capitalism was designed to enslave them. Messages from every major institution in society conditioned the poor to believe that unless the government pulled them out of poverty, they could not get out. That conditioning is one reason why so many people today are poverty-stricken amidst tremendous opportunities for economic prosperity. Remember that woman on Oprah who was convinced to her core that leaving welfare would mean her child would starve? This belief has become intrinsic to their worldview.

One example of this victimization attitude was revealed when I spoke about welfare reform at the University of North Carolina at Chapel Hill. During my discourse I suggested that, as the federal government moved to decline in its role of providing welfare services, the extended family should increase its role in helping their needy relatives. When I finished my presentation, a well-polished, very articulate black woman in the audience stood up and shouted, "What about my niece?" The woman explained that although she was college-educated and accomplished professionally, she was offended that I dared to suggest she share her home with her niece as opposed to the government providing subsidized housing. "Capitalism is a system of racism," she shouted and declared that without government intervention her niece was doomed.

Her niece, a sixteen-year-old unmarried mother, had been taught that her poverty was the result of historical prejudice and exploitation. She sat next to her aunt looking indignant yet helpless. After the program concluded, I talked with the niece and tried to stimulate a desire for financial independence apart from welfare. It was as if I was talking to a zombie. She insisted that any attempt to leave poverty was a waste of her time. "The white man ain't gonna let you git too far," she said. "This is his, and he always be there to keep me down."

Sadly, that poor girl really believed racism stood between her and financial freedom. Her aunt encouraged the niece's government dependency because she believed that successful blacks represented a few lucky exceptions to a racist rule. She lived in fear that her own success was at risk without federal oversight. Liberals have hijacked her history and have used it as a shackle.

Thirty-five years of Great Society social engineering have forced the disadvantaged to live under the control of the federal government. Politicians control their housing, food supply, schooling, wages, and transportation. A centralized government makes decisions about their childcare, healthcare, and retirement. It controls their reproduction through abortion and wants to control their deaths through euthanasia.

With the silent approval of religious organizations, the federal government has replaced religion as the answer for people in need. It is the perfect position from which liberal scholars and other social elitists have launched their assaults to redefine truth. The technical term for this position is "statism," but the modern term is "liberalism" and its nickname is "Uncle Sam."

As theologian R.C. Sproul explains in *Welfare Reformed: A Compassionate Approach*, statism is "a philosophy of government whereby the state is not only the final ruling authority but also the ultimate agency of redemption." This philosophy was long embraced by atheists, relativists, and supporters of socialism because it gave them the power to define justice, rights, and morality. Under statism, civil magistrates can question the integrity of religion and supplant its authority. Federal courts could reinterpret the First Amendment of the Constitution to place a wall of separation between the Church and the State. Politicians and judges have sole power to dictate, mandate, and regulate all public matters. Civil magistrates can put the federal government in charge of all matters of family, commerce, and society. Americans can forget about their problems. The government has it under control.

Under the dictates of Uncle Sam, the risks of life become engineering problems, and the goal of government is to eliminate those problems. The federal solution to poverty is the redistribution of wealth via disproportionate taxes on the wealthy. The plan is ingenious really: identify the need for atonement, demonize the people with the most money, tax them unfairly, and if anyone complains, say they are racist or heartless or both.

Uncle Sam has developed a sophisticated poverty plantation, operated by a federal government, overseen by bureaucrats, protected by media elite, and financed by the taxpayers. The only difference between this plantation and the slave plantations of the antebellum South is perception. If anyone works their way off of the plantation and denounces it, they are called "uppity" or "sellout" or even "Uncle Tom." Instead of a physical beating, defectors are ostracized in the public forum. Blacks have been repeatedly warned both publicly and privately that to leave the government's poverty plantation will mean a life of isolation from their family and abandonment by their peers.

4

The Welfare State

Blame it on poverty. Blame it on racism. A person can come up with all of the excuses in the world for why we need to perpetuate a robust welfare system. When Franklin D. Roosevelt began implementing the sweeping reforms that would pave the way for our current welfare system, the moral and financial state of the nation was on a steady decline. The ravages of a worldwide depression had to be mitigated, and to his credit, FDR carried our nation through one of the most difficult periods of its second hundred years. Could he have foreseen the monster he was creating? People were desperate. How could he imagine the deplorable living conditions, substandard education, inner city riots, and the assassinations of political and religious leaders which would come to characterize the very class of people the system was designed to help?

Would FDR have made changes to his legislative agenda if he had known that in a few short decades all authority, institutions, and absolutes would be questioned; that word would be out that some of America's founders owned slaves; that the character of these founders would be on trial and liberals would conclude that their flawed nature disqualified their concepts of self-government; and worst of all, that human nature would arrogantly be labeled an engineering problem that could be fixed by forcing equality and conformity?

A study of history suggests he did not intend for either political party to hijack the system by fostering the idea of white people paying for the elimination of negative socio-environmental and economic forces. Neither did he think a centralized government could improve the lives of the poor and thereby atone for the sins of America's past.

At face value, the thinking seems compassionate; if you pass laws to raise wages for the poor and lower their rent, if you give generously to help support the jobless and homeless, you can assist in their flight from poverty and alleviate much of the distress of institutional racism. This kind of compassion, however, does not take human nature into account and is therefore ignorant of the most volatile part of the equation: uninformed compassion often hurts more than it helps. With the best of intentions, the champions of our welfare system believed they could make government the beneficent source of supply for the beleaguered masses. They were wrong.

WELFARE TODAY

Sondra was born in 1980. Her dad was a postal worker, and her mom worked on and off at a variety of entry-level jobs. When her mom got mixed up in drugs and broke up the marriage, Sondra bounced between the two homes. Before long her grades in school reflected the chaos. If we defined poverty in the context of our nation's wealth and standards of living then Sondra would be classified as poor. If we used a political definition to describe the demographics of her living conditions then Sondra would be classified as having grown up in the ghetto. If the teacher's union were making its classic case to whine for more federal funds for education they would use Sondra's high school experience to stir up a collective sense of guilt. Even so, does it necessarily follow that, at the ripe old age of twenty-one, Sondra's place on the welfare roll is really a result of racism and poverty?

Sondra did not learn how to read. Without the benefit of a formal test, I would estimate her literacy at about third grade level. In the four years I have known her, sometimes I have had her jot down a note or try to read a few street signs or a menu so that she will get some practice. But frankly most of our conversations revolve around my attempts to adjust Sondra's attitude toward the responsibilities of life. A compassionate liberal might expect her to call me mean-spirited, or something worse; but she doesn't, even though I unfailingly push her toward the harder path of self-reliance. How do those who promote victimology explain why Sondra keeps soliciting my opinions?

Sondra got pregnant during high school and had an abortion. Sondra got pregnant again right after high school and had a baby boy. When she told the father of the child she was pregnant, he called it a "keep a nigga baby," a common phrase used by inner city men who have no intention of taking care of their responsibilities. It is used by a deadbeat dad as an epithet to keep the woman in check, to let her know he is convinced she got pregnant on purpose as a means to keep him in her life. *Ah, young love.* It warms the heart.

Although there is a small percentage within the lazy poor who would deliberately have a baby just to go on welfare, the majority of women in this situation, including Sondra, simply got caught up in sexual lust. Their pregnancy is the result of poor judgment and uncontrolled impulses. The deadbeat dad is in jail now anyway. He got arrested for shaking another baby to death—a baby he had fathered who was two months older than Sondra's baby. Most of Sondra's grief over that tragic event was that the boyfriend didn't tell her "some other bitch was carrying his child while he was with me." She's "over wanting to hook up with him" but gave him the following advice: "That hood rat set you up, and you should cut her off for good when you get out." She moved in with his mother for a while to keep tabs on his progress, but his mother wanted her to pay two hundred dollars rent. She told her to forget it.

The only thing that worries Sondra today is that Republicans are trying to change the welfare system again. When she went to apply for "her money" they told her that Republicans had changed the rules and she would only be able to get help for two years. "Look what you did, Star," she told me referring to my work in welfare reform. "Now they're making me find a job or go back to school. Ain't no job gonna pay me enough, beside how am I gonna git there when that car my daddy gave me is a piece of junk?" Sondra actually bought the lie that she is a victim. The welfare benefits that Sondra complains she has to receive with new restrictions and limitations include cash grants, housing, food stamps, childcare services, and medical care—everything a welfare slave needs to survive on Uncle Sam's plantation.

UNCLE SAM'S PROGRAMS

When most people think of welfare, they think of what for decades was called Aid to Families with Dependent Children (AFDC), which the Personal Responsibility and Work Opportunity Reconciliation Act of 1996, the law known as "welfare reform," changed to Temporary Assistance for Needy Families (TANF). This program is means-tested and the most appropriate program to look at when describing the type of welfare Sondra wants to get at the same level as her unmarried yet pregnant predecessors.

Due to the enormity of the welfare system in our country, with all the facets of its programs and sub-programs, it would be easy to get bogged down in the minutiae. We will therefore move briskly through the salient details, focusing primarily on the programs for which Sondra qualified immediately upon hearing the news about her new bundle of joy.

Temporary Assistance for Needy Families (TANF)

AFDC by any other name is still welfare. AFDC began in 1935 as part of the Social Security Act. The program provides cash payments to children of families whose fathers or mothers are absent, incapacitated, deceased, or unemployed. Each state determines its own benefit levels and eligibility requirements within certain federal restrictions. Both the state and the feds pay for the programs with the federal government averaging about 55 percent of the funding, according to Michael Tanner in his Cato Institute book, *The End of Welfare: Fighting Poverty in the Civil Society.*

The changes made by the Welfare Reform Act of 1996 combined AFDC and the Job Opportunities and Basic Skills program under one umbrella called TANF—so the new goal of welfare was to move the recipients of the services toward financial independence. This 1996 act of the Republican Congress was signed into law by then President Bill Clinton and allowed the states to administer their own cash assistance programs, with a few federal restrictions, which the federal government would fund through block grants. TANF law restricts the amount of time that a welfare recipient can collect benefits, which is the part Sondra hates most. The law says she can only collect cash grants for two years, five years over a lifetime. Sondra also must work a predetermined number of hours or be in school in order to get the money.

Job Opportunities and Basic Skills Training (JOBS)

The dead horse program known as JOBS was established in 1988 to replace the failing work incentive (WIN) program set in place at the beginning of the Great Society. The JOBS program was administered at the federal level and included services such as remedial education to achieve a basic literacy level, job skills training, and job readiness activities—essential training one might expect to learn in high school. Job development and job placement were also a part of this liberal dream that became a nightmare to the business community.

JOBS was redundant, often conflicted with the requirements of other welfare programs, and could do nothing to force welfare recipients to take advantage of its services. This program was combined into the TANF program of 1996 so the people behind this national attempt to "end welfare as we know it" could showcase a welfare-to-work philosophy. Under new law, Sondra must submit to a variety of job training and educational services provided through the bureaucracy of the old JOBS program to find work or obtain work skills while she receives cash benefits from welfare.

Emergency Assistance to Needy Families with Children (EANF)

Sondra qualified for this federal program because she refused to live with a relative or family friend. She was offered the opportunity, but when the rules of the house were laid down, Sondra opted to seek out emergency assistance for a housing voucher available to the evicted or homeless. EANF consists of cash payments and other in-kind payments to help people in distress. The original intent of this relic of the Social Security Act was to give states permission to provide emergency assistance to needy families with children for no more than thirty days per year.

Most emergency assistance is given because of natural disasters, although other qualifying causes include eviction, homelessness, utility shutoff, loss of employment or strike, and emergency medical needs. The New Deal promoters of the Depression era did not anticipate that the term "emergency" would be twisted into an entitlement for an apartment if one chose to list Uncle Sam in the paternity box on the welfare questionnaire.

Section 8 Housing

Housing Assistance Payments were created by section 8 of the Housing Act of 1937. Families qualify if the household income falls below 50 percent of the median family income for a family of that size in the county in which they reside. TANF payments are counted as income, but food stamps and other forms of public assistance are not, which means that all TANF recipients qualify to be placed on a waiting list for section 8 housing or for a place in one of the federal government's three thousand housing projects operated by the Department of Housing and Urban Development (HUD).

Sondra is on the list for both, and whichever becomes available first will determine where she will live next. For now, she and her six-month-old baby are bouncing between the apartments of different friends. Naturally, she prefers the section 8 because it offers more neighborhood choices.

Food Stamps

The next time the person in front of you at the grocery store is using these vouchers to purchase food or other items, take a moment to look very discreetly at the attractive layout of the food stamp itself. Unlike most paper money, they are crisp, clean, and they come in a variety of colors to differentiate their value. They are so cute and creative; it's hard to imagine they have the power to drain personal freedom out of a living, breathing human being.

Food stamps are available to help subsidize low-income households in their efforts to maintain an adequate diet. The program operates in all U.S. territories, and the federal government sets benefit levels and eligibility standards, which can vary state by state. The U.S. Department of Agriculture determines what an adequate diet is, and the amount of food stamps one receives varies depending on household income and the cost of food in his or her state. Recipients of TANF are automatically eligible for food stamps.

Sondra has no real complaints against this program because although she only receives food stamps valued at about $245 a month, welfare doesn't restrict what types of food products she can purchase. She can always trade a few stamps with a friend to buy the non-food grocery items that don't qualify, such as beer or cigarettes. And for additional food items she also gets special assistance.

Special Supplemental Food Program for Women, Infants, and Children (WIC)

WIC is part of the Child Nutrition Act of 1966 that provides specialized food assistance and nutritional screening for pregnant and postpartum women and their infants, as well as for low-income children up to the age of five. The chief complaint from women such as Sondra about WIC is that the voucher is bulky and can only be used for specific items. The actual food purchases differ according to the age of the children and whether the mother is pregnant or nursing, but generally the WIC voucher is for milk, cheese, eggs, infant formula, cereals, and fruit and vegetable juices.

Perhaps you have noticed some WIC labels up and down the aisles at your grocery store lately. These labels are a new way for the government to more accurately regulate the supplemental value of the program. Public pressure against welfare waste made it hard for liberals to protect this program as "nutritional" when most of the cereal purchased was more like candy than health food.

Child Care for Recipients of TANF

Under this program, all TANF recipients receive free day care. The law allows states to guarantee day care by direct provision or through the use of vouchers or reimbursements. All TANF recipients who need child care in order to go to school, work, or training are eligible. Since TANF recipients are required to participate in one or more of these three activities, this means that federal law qualifies all TANF recipients to obtain care from a state provider or use a certificate that is payable for child care from the provider of their choice.

When the welfare recipient is working at an income level above that provided through TANF, the childcare grant might be adjusted to a slid-ing schedule set by the state, which means the parent will have to pay the difference. Sondra recently spoke of crossing this line and then hav-ing to pay for childcare she says she cannot afford. The few times I have tried to help her understand mathematically that when she makes more money than the "free qualification" level allows, she will actually have a net gain of $200 monthly after paying for the childcare, she shrugs and yells, "The hell with it, why can't they just mind their own business?" The one time I did respond to her ranting by saying "welfare *is* their business," she cursed me and stormed out. So most of the time I try to limit the sarcasm when she visits.

Medicaid

The Medicaid program, Title XIX of the Social Security Act, was begun in 1965 and is the nation's primary health care program for the needy. It covers low-income adults and children, but the majority of Medicaid spending covers a variety of services for the elderly and dis-abled that are not included in the Medicare program. Like TANF, Medicaid is administered by the states within broad federal guidelines. Funding is divided between the federal and state governments with the feds averaging 57 percent of the costs, according to Michael Tanner.

All major medical considerations are covered under this program for those who qualify. All TANF recipients qualify, including Sondra. While states have the option of paying for a few additional services, such as mental health, dental care, eyeglasses, or prescription drugs, most states pay for them all.

The fact is that the welfare system is much bigger than these few programs that are a part of Sondra's reality today. There are more than seventy-seven major federal welfare programs, most of which are built on other programs for which Sondra will later qualify should she con-tinue her current path.

MORAL BANKRUPTCY

In our attempt to blame poverty on prejudice, we have taught the poor to be prejudiced against the basic values necessary to sustain a free and civil society. We've taught them that it is okay to become dependent pawns of Uncle Sam. We've taught them there are no real absolutes to the human condition—except perhaps that the highest value in life is to acquire things. This is the godless materialism of the social planners hard at work. Life's definition of success has been denigrated to the lowest common denominator of personal power and personal wealth. In fact, many Americans assume that moral boundaries to govern human nature are subjective and the concepts of right and wrong can be navigated without a religious framework. This idea of moral relativism reflected in society has left our nation in desperate need of ethical order. People like Sondra are simply listening to and living out the new rules.

The old rules were predicated on the notion that if a man worked hard, bought a piece of property, got married before producing children, and saved or invested some money, he and his family would be secure. Civil government was primary, and its main role was to protect that man's work, his property, and his family by establishing a civil order based upon the laws of God, handed down primarily through the Jewish Tanakh and the Christian Old and New Testaments. In the Declaration of Independence, America's founding fathers stated that each person is endowed by the Creator with the fundamental rights of life, liberty, and the pursuit of happiness. They provided the framework for the protection of these rights in the Constitution.

The new rules insisted morality could be self-defined depending on one's circumstances, environment, experiences, culture, economics, or personal choice. "You cannot legislate morality" is the sound bite thrown around by those demanding autonomy and liberation from the religious roots of law. Political groups such as the ACLU and Americans United for the Separation of Church and State have precipitated major legal battles to ensure that any vestige of religion is removed from public property or public discourse, and most importantly from public education.

The decisions that I made in my younger years clearly show what can happen to an individual when attempting autonomy with undefined ethics and without moral law or transcendent values. Granted, most people do not naturally gravitate to the lowest value system as Sondra or I did. People who believe they have a lot to lose generally are less inclined toward morally bankrupt decisions because the personal cost in lost social status and self-esteem is too high. What so many fail to realize is that self-centeredness is the cornerstone of moral bankruptcy.

To behave amorally, you must merely be convinced to act in your own interest to the exclusion of all else. If you believe there are no God-given moral absolutes, morality becomes subjective—to each his own. We have only societal mores and human wisdom to guide us. History has consistently shown us where that wisdom leads. A hundred years ago, aborting an unborn child was a heinous crime. Now we are "wiser" and more "civilized," so we offer abortion on demand. As Randy Stonehill sang, "It's okay to murder babies, but we've got to save the whales." Depending on whose numbers you use, between forty and forty-five million unborn children have been aborted since the *Roe v. Wade* decision in 1973. No matter the defense of a woman's right to choose, that's at minimum 10 percent of our current population—tens of millions of young Americans who never saw the light of day, unless they survived long enough to see it briefly from the bottom of a dumpster. Wise and civilized indeed.

Without transcendent values, life derives meaning from acquisition—of things, of people, of status. Bring in an army of advertisers to tell us we deserve the most expensive car, the biggest house, the largest financial portfolio, the most prestigious career, and a hard body to share with whomever we want. Give them a media machine to rival any in the world, and the means to assault our senses 24-7,

and a case can be made that the enslavement of our willing population extends far beyond the welfare system. Karl Marx said religion is
the opiate of the masses, but we are systematically replacing religion
with media in our country. And before you quote any statistics on
church attendance, answer this: for every person who attended
church this past week, if you compared their religious activity to their
media consumption, which number would be higher? Without getting
into a discussion of moral content on television, how many of us
would confess to guilty pleasures in our viewing or listening choices?
In fairness, some of our moral outrage should be directed at ourselves.

So, if the social landscape is so complex, and so many issues that
used to be black and white now seem gray, what's a poor youngster
with limited education and limited access supposed to do with the new
standards and rules? Spend twenty years in school so they too can
acquire things? If "he who dies with the most toys wins," as the bumper
sticker says—and society affirms—why shouldn't a kid being taught by
the media, his leaders, and his educational establishment that values are
neutral just go out and "get mine" today? What possible argument could
we offer that would stop them from killing for power, stealing for prestige, or having a baby to get paid? For the morally bankrupt, the battle
of ideas is already lost. There can be no appeal to a higher nature
because it is excluded. There can be no appeal to reason because self-
ish needs reign supreme. The only way to control their behavior when
it exceeds societal boundaries is through the threat and use of force.
Again, so wise and civilized.

It seems many of those heralded as the most noble and accomplished in our society are the quickest to defend self-defined values
and boundaries. They attribute the failures of those less fortunate to
uncontrollable external forces, negating personal culpability for their
actions. Coincidentally, they indulge in feelings of superiority, as they
consider all other less prosperous individuals as members of an infe-

rior or lower class.

Look at the boundaries governing human sexuality as an example. This is where I repeatedly made damaging choices and demonstrated egregiously poor judgment. The same is true for Sondra and a high percentage of those living on welfare today. It is this area, perhaps more than any other, where a value-neutral attitude in our society has created the environment for poverty to skyrocket and also escalated the opportunities for government socialism to thrive.

Prior to the sexual revolution of the sixties, the common culture still had a moral sense that sexual intimacy was reserved for a husband and his wife. The old rule was that stepping outside of this boundary and becoming involved in adultery, fornication, or incest would bring not only public shame but also the weight of civil condemnation under a rule of law which viewed these as irresponsible, sinful, and oftentimes destructive acts.

Under the old rules, my sexual behavior would have subjected my family to public disgrace. In addition, I would have either been a financial burden upon them or the family of the man who impregnated me. Now, along comes Uncle Sam with my get-out-of-jail-free welfare card, and like magic I'm spared from the natural consequences of my reckless behavior. After all, disgrace and personal responsibility are so uncivilized, one might even say cruel and unusual, for an "enlightened" society.

I am not one to espouse grand conspiracy theories, but there are some disturbing developments in American sociology that pose some interesting questions. A pattern of deliberate, gradual moral erosion seems to characterize the liberal policies of the Left over the past forty years. If you were determined to control a population with a Judeo-Christian set of values, who believed they were endowed by their Creator with certain inalienable rights, your plans of conquest would have to include a method for assaulting those values, for they are the bedrock of the populace you wish to control. God and His

87

book must be replaced by something more malleable. Look for chinks in the armor. Do you see them? Grant absolution from responsibility, offer new definitions for moral absolutes, and when opposition rises up, confer a collective sense of guilt. That's a very good place to start. This nation has the bloodguilt of countless people of African descent, ripped from their homes, beaten, raped, and enslaved. Your ancestors perpetrated barbarous acts against a defenseless people, and we won't even talk about the Native Americans. Now these people are suffering again, ignored, ghettoized, and if you have a shred of human decency, you will do something about it. But wait! Do not despair. Your government has a solution, a compassionate solution, and all you have to do is pay for it. What a relief. Please pay no attention to the swelling ranks and budget of the federal government. It's all perfectly natural.

Now that the government is growing and people are beginning to believe that the answers lie in government subsidies and not faith in God or reliance on community, we must assault their most basic assumptions about human nature; for in the elevation of mankind, God is vanquished. Sin? What an antiquated concept. Get rid of it. Adultery is against the law? Ridiculous. It may be wrong, but who's to say? At the very least it should be decriminalized. Homosexuality? Don't call it sexual deviance, even though only a fool would say it does not violate the natural order. Call it sexual preference. Pedophilia? Well, I suppose we have to draw the line somewhere, at least for now. Let's call them warped and keep those laws on the books. For now.

I honestly don't believe there is a secret society that thinks this way, carefully plotting the demise of our nation. Most likely, a nation disillusioned by the ravages of a world war and the Great Depression began questioning their notions of God and His provision. This was the real chink in the armor, exploited by liberal intellectuals since the late 1940s. A whole segment of our society shrugged off the shackles of traditional morality and began testing the boundaries. When opposed, they would shrink back briefly and then begin pushing on those boundaries again. Remember when pornography meant *Playboy*? I wonder what Thomas Jefferson would have put in the Constitution if he had foreseen the explosion of filth on the Internet.

The sexual revolution was a natural outflow of this abandonment of traditional values. "Free love"—sounds harmless, doesn't it?—was the next natural step, for sexual desire is one of the most difficult to keep in line. If we can redefine it, we don't have to fight it anymore. Again, *what a relief.* What's darkly amusing is that the only thing the people in the sexual revolution succeeded in proving was that traditional values were not just an effort to spoil everyone's fun. Sex actually produces unwanted pregnancy? What a shock. I guess we have to get it under control by killing the children after they are conceived. Self-control? What an outdated idea. Throw it on the same pile with sin. What's this upswing in sexually transmitted disease? That never happened before. Better put the doctors on it. Abstinence? Throw it on the pile. Well, wait a sec. Set it aside, and we'll look at it if absolutely nothing else works with these new diseases. Monogamy? Put it on the pile with abstinence. What do you mean divorce rates are skyrocketing? It couldn't have any-thing to do with adultery. People are just learning they don't have to be bound by the uncivilized old ways anymore. Better make it easier to get a divorce, or we're going to overload the judicial system. What do you mean our children are in gangs and are having children themselves and are abusing drugs? How could this have happened? Don't they have parents? Oh, right. Well, if everything looked as hopeless as it does to them, I guess I'd want to do drugs and sleep around too. Better give them condoms. The drugs we can combat with commercials. Yeah, that'll work.

Atheists and agnostics are welcome to their opinions—this is still a free country—but the evidence is quite clear that most of our social ills can be traced back to the systematic breakdown of morality, the movement away from traditional values with personal responsibility to a system of self-determination and no moral absolutes. Study after study has proven that children do better in a two-parent home with a mother and a father, yet the media persists in trying to promote acceptance of "non-traditional" families. Books like *Heather Has Two Mommies* and *Daddy's Roommate*, while not in the mainstream, have been recommended to certain schools on the Left Coast.

Our decisions have consequences. No matter what your favorite sitcom says, like it or not, there is a promise made in any bed, unless the people using it are so unfeeling and calloused that sex means nothing but physical gratification. Why are we surprised when our children take automatic weapons and shoot up their schools? With our Gestapo interpretation of separation of Church and State, and the relentless propaganda of liberal ideology from the media and in classrooms, we have taken away their hope for a future. There is nothing to look forward to. Marriages don't last. The incredible bonding power of sexual union is cheapened and trivialized. The economy is failing. More wars are on the horizon. "Did you hear about that mother who drowned her kids in their car seats?" Most important, if there is no God or hope for an afterlife, then this is really all there is, and to paraphrase C.S. Lewis, you are a transitory and senseless contortion on the idiotic face of infinite matter.

Take away moral absolutes and any behavior becomes possible and defensible. As I approached puberty in the seventies, the feminists had already burned their bras, and the homosexuals were coming out of the closet. The ideas of sexual freedom imposed by these two movements had wormed their way into mainstream thought. Credible news sources, affluent writers, university scholars, professional associations, and even some church denominations began redefining what was normal. My amoral positions on sexual conduct were shaped by the ideas of free love that reached me through television, music, and the value-free sex education instruction taught during health class at my high school.

Little by little this counter-current to biblical truths and absolute guidelines had severely weakened the ability of society to respond to sexual deviance. Like slowly poisoning a well or rinsing all the milk out of a milk carton, the process is gradual. Sudden change is met with resistance, so the pressure must be steady, yet measured. Once the absolutes are successfully removed or sufficiently diluted, making one person's opinion as valid as the next, who's to say that a young woman cannot leave her newborn baby in the bathroom toilet and return to the prom dance floor? Who's to say that one cannot leave her baby in a trash dumpster when we allow millions to be placed there by medical professionals who swore under oath to preserve life? The war of ideas continues to rage, and despite liberal efforts to rinse the milky residue of moral absolutes from the carton of the national conscience, some milk remains, thanks to the efforts of decent people both in and out of the government.

People of good conscience must remain vigilant, however. The hydra has many heads, and every time it grows a new one, we must be standing ready to chop it off. I fear there will always be a new ballot measure promoting gay marriages, weakening traditional ones, or tearing down the Ten Commandments from a school or courtroom wall. By themselves, these may not be great beachheads in the grand scheme, but they represent a persistent effort to undermine all that is good, true, and praiseworthy about our country.

With moral responsibility thoroughly undermined, personal responsibility—simply taking charge for one's own decisions—also suffers. The welfare state as it's now constituted only facilitates this problem by cushioning what would otherwise be the hard smack of bad moral decisions. In one sense this seems compassionate. In a far more real sense, however, it's cruel because the welfare safety net deceives the poor about the destructive nature of their choices and prevents them from learning how to make good decisions.

SAFETY NETS

We hear the language of welfare safety nets all the time. Guaranteed healthcare. Abortion rights. Rent control. Sex education. Affirmative action. Public assistance. Minimum wage. Assisted suicide. Labor unions. Social Security.

In most public schools, learning this language is a mandatory requirement that takes priority over learning a foreign language, especially at the university level. Uncle Sam's plantation cannot run smoothly without conformity. Safety nets are government-coerced benefits provided to anyone who does not prepare for the unwanted results of their particular decisions or actions. The "village chiefs" of civil safety nets run the major civil rights organizations today. They have very vocal and imposing spokespersons in Congress and in the media. One is currently leading the charge for reparations in the House of Representatives. One is currently running for the Democratic nomination for the presidency. Others we hear from endlessly in the news bouncing from political rallies to corporate shakedowns.

Their chief line of offense is to litigate or instigate litigation against overt and covert racism as they define it. In addition to looking for racism behind every non-minority face or expression and in every home or neighborhood, every business or school, every public or private institution, every club, every church, every party or social gathering, they have created an entire industry around the perception of racism based on speech and, where possible, thoughts.

So it is also with the safety nets of welfare services. The village chiefs of welfare safety nets run the Democratic party today. They have very subtle yet intimidating spokespersons in academia and in the media. One is currently leading the charge for infanticide as a professor at Princeton University. One is currently considered the queen of television talk. Others rarely make the news as they tirelessly promote liberalism, socialism, and atheism.

They operate under a perceived mandate to manipulate the social trends of minorities and the poor for power, prestige, or political gain. In addition to looking for control over every growing portfolio, in every home or neighborhood, every business or school, every public or private institution, every club, every church, every party or social gathering, they have created an entire vocabulary around the politics of political correctness.

The village chiefs teach that the only higher authority worthy of submission is government. The political world of statism promises to replace the natural circumstances created by moral bankruptcy with safety nets. The safety net promise was warranted because moral relativism is intellectual narcissism, a love affair with the human intellect to the exclusion of the existence of God—or if you prefer, Shirley MacLaine standing on the beach shouting, "I am God! I am God!" As a result, so-called intellectuals would have us believe no problem exists that is beyond the ability of enlightened mankind to solve.

The answer of safety nets was a misguided attempt to cover up the social pathologies associated with the bad choices of the underprivileged. The doctrine of secular humanism (the belief that human nature is a question of science, not of ethics or religion) resulted from the unanticipated outcome of their belief that mankind does not have to answer to an infinite authority, and so the "unenlightened" began to cast off all moral restraints.

I remember the first time an acquaintance talked to me about breaking into a house to steal a television. He reasoned that "the system" was designed to keep people of color from having full access to the American dream. He reminded me of how few material possessions we blacks collectively owned. After all, he was from a very poor, broken home from which he ran away at the age of sixteen.

I said to myself, "Yeah, he's right! I have to share one bathroom with six others in my parents' home and (according to my village chiefs) that's not fair!"

He suggested the only way we would ever get ahead or "get ours" was to take it from someone else. Were we not just following the natural lead of our liberal Uncle Sam? We were simply redistributing on a more personal level. Don't worry about the prospect of getting busted. The village chiefs had already mastered their legal claim of safety nets for the ancestors of African slaves. Good and evil had nothing to do with my actions. I was the victim of a racist society. My crime was against three hundred years of slavery. The fact that African-Americans represented 40 percent of the two million prisoners simply proved that racism still dominated the criminal justice system, and this justified more personal redistribution of wealth through stealing, which necessitated more Johnny Cochrans to get us off the hook for our justifiable crimes.

I like what Penn State Professor Alan Kors said about the college madness for the Young America Foundation's College Lecture Series. He challenged schools to have the courage to advertise their mind game of politically correct indoctrination. He said an honest advertisement aimed at parents and prospective students should read, "This University believes that your sons and daughters are the racist, sexist, Eurocentric, homophobic progeny of a racist, sexist, homophobic, oppressive American society. For $25,000 per year, we shall assign rights unequally on a compensatory basis and undertake by coercion the moral and political enlightenment of your children."

A classroom of expanding minds has been a safe haven for the proponents of safety nets. Before the naivete and openness of students, village chiefs could easily disguise their elitism and superior humanity over the underprivileged by innocently asking, "But what if?" "What if racism keeps property owners from providing low rents?" "What if sexism keeps women trapped in Victorian marriages?" "What if Eurocentrism keeps schools from allowing minorities entrance?" "What if homophobia keeps AIDS patients from receiving available treatment?" "What if greed keeps corporations from paying livable wages or providing adequate healthcare or retirement benefits?"

The reason language codes and common political vocabulary encompass safety nets is because common sense runs counter to welfare protectionism. Take the analogy of the swimming pool.

We have swimming pools so people can swim. There is a shallow end and a deep end of the swimming pool. This allows all people regardless of their training to go into the water at their individual comfort level. Some will go into the shallow end and learn to swim. Some will go into the deep end because they already know how to swim. People choose to go into the area that reflects their personal desires and abilities.

One day, an advocate against drowning decides that the pool offers too much risk of drowning because it has a deep end. He calls on an advocate for swimming pool rights who in turn expresses that it is not fair some people must stay in the shallow end because they do not know how to swim while others have greater swimming privileges.

They hold a press conference and call on government to intervene for the shallow-enders. The public is alarmed as the media shows person after person being discriminated against because they do not know how to swim. Of course they exaggerate the problem by cutting between images of pools in the backyards of affluent neighborhoods and sobbing minority kids at the press conference that have never even been in a swimming pool.

Their political insider sees the press conference and goes on C-SPAN the next day to plead for a war on drowning. A congresswoman pressures her colleagues to pass a bill that designates a one-size-fits-all guarantee against drowning. The new law forces more taxes out of swimmers and non-swimmers to build a pool in every low-income neighborhood and mandates that all pools in the country must have no more than two feet of water so everyone can get in without drowning. Common sense tells John Q. Public that it is a stupid law, but we all know that John is really just trying to protect the pool in his all-white neighborhood. So the speech police must impress on John a new vocabulary in order not to cause offense since he is harboring racist feelings against the sobbing minority kids and wants to keep them out of his pool.

Of course John sees that with the new law no one can swim, not even the kids at the press conference crying about not knowing how to swim. That is because you are a racist, John. See how much trouble you cause by being a racist? How do you expect them to learn to swim and compete with your children when you have a pool at your home and they don't?

At some point, however, the politically correct rhetoric backfires against the liberal elite who coined it. The no-drowning advocates have done such a good job indoctrinating their ranks that, if John utters one more insensitive word, taxpayers could end up with a commission to study equal access to pool services that could lead to a federal Department for Swimming Pool Security. Then the rest of the public will become so fed-up they will vote the no-drowning crowd out of office. They wouldn't like that.

It's been hard enough for the speech police to stop or discredit the conservatives who say rugged individualism should inspire each to make responsible choices for positive outcomes. Trying to censor the Rush Limbaughs of the world without appearing hypocritical has drained quite a bit of their intellectual resources and strained their credibility. The last thing they want is to drive more of their ranks into the arms of the conservatives.

The welfare system had some of its teeth taken out in 1996 under the welfare reform put forward by the Republicans in Congress, but the monster is far from dead. Time limits and work requirements are a step in the right direction, but the culture of Uncle Sam's plantation is fed

by the misguided policies of the Left. As long as there are liberal ideo-
logues in the halls of power, there is a long, hard battle ahead for those
of us committed to seeing poor people emancipated from a paternalistic system that robs them of their initiative, their freedom, and ultimately their hope for the future.

5

Undermining Family

No institution fights poverty better than the family—a refuge in the hard fight from privation to wealth. But Uncle Sam's plantation weakens the family in two primary ways:

1. Removing the man's responsibility to care for his family. If he wants to split the scene with his buddies or a new girlfriend, the State is there to pick up the tab, freeing him of accountability.

2. Freeing women from having to face up to their end of the responsibilities. If a woman gets pregnant out of wedlock, Uncle Sam will pick up the bill for the abortion; if she decides to keep the child, he'll buy the groceries. (And Sam is better than a husband because he doesn't leave his socks in the living room after work or beer caps on the kitchen counter.)

This alone would be bad enough, but, whether by aim or accident, Uncle Sam works in concert with various cultural pressures to further undermine the family, beginning with the re-characterization of the roles of both men and women in society. First, we will look at the women.

FEMINISM:
THE BIG LIE

"Level the library," the feminists chanted. "Tear that building down!" The W.E.B. DuBois Library at the University of Massachusetts was the only high rise on the main campus grounds. About fourteen stories high and surrounded by trees, the building sported a beautiful pond and sitting benches, with all the other school buildings sprinkled about. The landscaping had the type of serene aura that makes New England so popular.

No one jogging or relaxing the fall evening I was scheduled to lecture at the school seemed to have any problem whatsoever with the atmosphere or with the library. It was buzzing with students going in and out, cramming for tests, taking notes, or surfing the Internet. I later found out, however, that several of the feminist students were very upset with the library. They felt that because of its size and location in the middle of the smaller campus buildings, the building was a phallic symbol and hence represented male dominance and needed to be torn down.

What insanity could prompt a group of otherwise logical people to advocate the destruction of millions of dollars worth of property based on a silly idea that the shape of the building represented male oppression and dominance? It didn't take a brain surgeon to figure out the insanity of modern feminism—stating that men are oppressors, marriage is prostitution, and money is power—was clearly to blame. Which is not to say that the feminists didn't have a reason to be angry.

Since the dawn of time, women have been beaten, degraded, and subjugated by men. Even today, in less civilized countries, women are sold into slavery, treated as servants and property, and in some regions subjected to genital mutilation. There are still countries where a male member of her family can kill a woman without a trial if she brings dishonor to the family. The modern construct of husband and wife working as a team is a product of mid-to-late twentieth century Western culture.

But it is the application of this anger in the form of damaging, self-defeating policies that continues to threaten our society. Feminists bend over backward to remove a nurturing mother from the family unit and then wonder why male children grow up hating women. Most working moms are not able to give adequate quality time to their children—even the term "quality time" is a cop out, because it presupposes the lack of quantity time. Not every child neglected in this way grows up to be a mass murderer like Klebold and Harris of Columbine infamy, but emotional damage is still inflicted and re-inflicted when mothers go AWOL on their kids. Despite the facts, feminists keep ignoring the studies and the mounting evidence of damage to our children—after all, it's every woman's right to join the workforce.

So, the feminist movement on campus was demanding the tall—and square—library come down. I immediately recognized the lie of feminism at work here because the same thinking was behind my earlier drive to live a carefree and promiscuous sexual lifestyle.

The sexual revolution of the sixties was no accidental culmination of random events. The modern assault on marriage began in the late 1800s, a natural follow-up to the Enlightenment period, which was supported by liberals, socialists, and other secular groups and gained strength in the nineteenth century. The problem was bad enough even then for Pope Leo XIII to come out in support of Christian marriage on February 10, 1880, denouncing civil marriages and divorces and reaffirming the Church's rightful control of marriage. The slow, steady move of society toward secularism continued through the beginning of World War I. The ensuing decade—the roaring twenties—marked the first major society-wide eruption of moral deterioration in our country. Women were becoming more aggressive, and a society recovering from the greatest war to date was questioning many of its founding principles. This was the decade of women gaining the right to vote,

UNCLE SAM'S PLANTATION

Creationism on the stand in the Scopes "monkey trial," the failure of Prohibition, and the rise of organized crime, Al Capone, and Bonnie and Clyde.

Though groups around the world pushed for equality, early twentieth century efforts by feminists in America were met mostly with scorn and ridicule. The feminists quickly learned what every radical social group learns: when you push society too hard, society pushes back. It was not until 1953 that another major feminist milestone appeared on the scene. *The Second Sex*, written by French existentialist, atheist, and abortion advocate Simone de Beauvoir, was the first feminist manifesto calling for women's independence. Once again, a society shaken to its foundations by another world war was grasping for understanding and truth. De Beauvoir advocated freedom of choice as mankind's premier value, asserting that acts of good increase freedom and bad ones limit freedom. It looks good on paper, especially if you think God is an oppressive construct of a paternalistic society and you are able to ignore the ugly facts of human nature.

Less the laughingstock it was at first, feminism began to gain some intellectual acceptance in the fifties. In 1961, the first oral contraceptive—the Pill—was developed, making it possible for the first time for the reproductive consequences of sexual intercourse to be consistently avoided. In 1964, *The Feminine Mystique* by Betty Friedan was a bestseller and hence a pretty good indicator that feminism was making progress. In 1964, Title VII of the Civil Rights Act was passed, prohibiting discrimination in hiring on the basis of sex.

Feminists of the mid-twentieth century were given to the most wild and unsupportable statements about the role of women in society, and yet the liberal and educational elite embraced their philosophy with gusto. Why? They had a common goal: the deconstruction of the family to make way for a socialist utopia. In 1971 the Equal Rights Amendment (ERA) passed the House of Representatives. The following year, the Senate passed the ERA by a vote of 84-8. The amendment was sent to the states for ratification, which never came. So, once again, despite efforts to push their ideals on an unsuspecting public, the Left lost to the will of the American people. This is why you see such contempt for the public in certain liberal quarters. Every now and then, the veneer of civility slips, and you catch a Leftist politician saying, in essence, that the American people are too stupid to know what's good for them. (When you hear these things—when you hear a Tom Daschle raving about the mindless cattle who allowed the Republicans to take over congress— just smile, because it means we are winning, and they can't stand it.)

On January 22, 1973, one of the darkest days for the American justice system, the Supreme Court ruled that a woman's decision to have a first-trimester abortion was between her and her doctor, in the case of *Roe v. Wade*. A similar case, *Doe v. Bolton*, also decided in 1973, essentially legalized abortion throughout the entire nine months. Now, it is legally every woman's right to kill, and many have chosen to exercise this right, to the tune of over thirty million dead by the end of the twentieth century.

In the thirty years since *Roe v. Wade*, feminists have continued to make inroads into American culture; some of them have been good (as in the case of Sally Ride becoming the first American woman in space) and others not (as in the appointment of feminist Ruth Bader Ginsburg to the Supreme Court). The feminists wage their war on many fronts, subjecting girls who play with Barbie dolls to ridicule and encouraging boys not to be boys but play gentle, "civilized" games that fly in the face of their masculinity.

American society continues to keep the most radical feminists at bay, but their assault is ongoing, pushing now at the grade school level, gradually getting their proponents into teaching positions and political positions and content to wait for another generation that is less resistant, whenever that time will come. Make no mistake—*the only thing necessary for their agenda to triumph is for good men and women to give up the fight.*

UNPAID WHORES AND OLD MAIDS

By the time I had moved into my teenage years, the feminist movement was in full gear. Thousands of women had burned their bras, left their husbands, and entered careers. God was no longer to be referred to as "He." The words "provider" and "husband" were also being redefined. The term "father" went no further than the legal and biological whims of the mother, and under the guise of reproductive rights any unborn life she may have been carrying could be destroyed thanks to the "freedom" afforded by the infamous *Roe v. Wade* decision.

Authority had taken on new meaning. So why would I, or anyone primed for Uncle Sam's plantation, ever consider discipline regarding sexuality and family life? I believed the lies of the feminist movement. "Marriage has nothing to do with romantic expressions or sexual fulfillment. It is actually a form of bondage. The story of Cinderella was written by a man to keep us girls under Victorian oppression." "But now there is an alternative," the enlightened of the feminist movement said. "We know better: You can have real freedom through obtaining a career and taking over all leadership from men. Marriage is really a form of male domination to keep us women subjected to them and dependent on them. It is actually another form of prostitution and slavery."

Slavery? Now, there's a divisive, emotionally charged word. But being black, it made sense to me, despite the obvious intent of race baiting. So, I decided marriage would not be part of my future, and I was not alone. While this mode of thinking may have been unusual in the forties and fifties, by the seventies there were millions of other girls thinking just like me.

Who taught us to think this way? A relatively small but determined band of college degreed, career accomplished, financially competitive, single or divorced, cohabiting or swinging female leaders. Why would it cross my mind to question their motives? The radical call to "question authority" only referred to "conservative authority," and the thought that these women might be horribly deluded or even outright deceitful was never on my screen. It wasn't until after my fourth trip to one of their "safe, legal, rare" abortion clinics that I even began to question their credibility and whether they were really looking out for my best interests as a female.

When I debated on the subject of "Feminism in the '90s" at Hillary Clinton's alma mater, Wellesley College in Boston, the subject of marriage was on trial. Many of today's colleges are social laboratories for students to be filled with wild and ridiculous notions in regards to gender roles. It was obvious just walking onto the campus that a conservative perspective wasn't going to receive a warm reception. The art museum contained derogatory paraphernalia about religion and men. There were big "wanted" posters of Christian Coalition leaders Dr. Pat Robertson and Ralph Reed hanging in the entry of the assembly hall. Although the campus was magnificent in décor and scenic ambiance, I sensed hostility against men in the conversations of many of the students at this all-female school. Several openly discussed their lesbianism, while others seemed obsessed with destroying what they called "the male power structure in America."

I opened my allotted three minutes with this statement: "I believe that radical feminism has created the environment for illegitimacy and poverty to skyrocket." At first, the silence in the room was intense. Then, my opponent, one of the feminist instructors at the school, stated that more education and more income were the solutions to poverty and that illegitimacy was a male term used to suppress women into marriage. The all-female audience broke out into an ovation at her statements, and then they mocked my reply that marriage was a legitimate option for female fulfillment and security. From personal experience I asked, "What about the welfare mom? Would you rather leave her subjected to housing projects, food stamps, and a menial check from the government than offer marriage as an alternative?" Their response was predictable: "No, pay for her to go to college so she won't need a man."

In the March 4, 2002, *Cornell Review,* Joseph Sabia makes the point that college-age women are encouraged to have sex when they want, with whomever they want. He rejects the notion that women can have a civilizing effect on men. The men think this is a fine idea. In the old days to have sex on demand with no commitment or consequences, men had to go to a whorehouse and pay good money for it. Now the whores are giving it away for free in dormitories across America and calling it sexual freedom. Empty-headed young women with parents who apparently had no clue how to set appropriate boundaries for their daughters have been fooled by liberals and feminists into giving up the only power they ever had over men: the power to withhold sex to ensure a long term relationship through marriage and a legacy for their union in the form of a strong family unit and children. Feminism has created a legion of unpaid whores who have abandoned God and family for the bondage of heartless, soulless physical union. They have given away the farm and gotten nothing in return. They have been sold a lie by leaders who want them free of the strength of a family unit, so they can be more easily manipulated. But that's only part of the problem.

In March 2003, *Newsweek* magazine reported that according to the 2000 census, 47 percent of black women age 30-34 have never married, compared to 10 percent of white women. The discovery was part of a March 2003 article on "The Black Gender Gap." The article also reported that 65 percent more young black women go to college than black men. It looked at the question of whether black women are now overqualified to find and marry a black man. One interviewee, a lawyer, said, "I figured that as I made more money and got the education that's required to get a good job, that that would automatically make it easier for me to find someone. But it's really been the opposite." The four professional women interviewed at the end of the article all agreed. One said that while she does very well financially, she does not want to be alone. Another said, "You can get a dog, keep yourself busy . . . keep yourself tired," but she wonders if she "will die in a room all by myself." Another went as far as to say, "I want babies and love in my life." Well, well, well. Apparently the feminist lie has backfired on black women.

"There are all kinds of other options," the immoral elite has told these women for the last thirty years. "You don't need a husband to help you achieve your goals. There are other alternatives to having your emotional, physical, and even spiritual needs met. A husband will only hinder your quest for self-fulfillment." Black women were more susceptible to the feminist promise of a brighter future because their communities were in economic ruin. The incomes of black men were at the bottom of the totem pole, so black women invested their youth in the rhetoric that has now left them unfulfilled old maids. I have spoken to a lot of career-bound college women who have reasoned away this obvious conflict between their beliefs and the facts on display in their neighborhoods. They begin with a strained attempt to prove that they want nothing to do with relationships and love, for they have been taught to compete with men professionally, to be accomplished financially, and to postpone marriage. This intellectual turmoil results in an attempt to ignore nature and cheat their biological needs. It's only after years of negligence that the "I can do anything a man can do" woman finds out that her hidden desire for the Cinderella dream didn't die, and now she's forty and without a husband and with little hope.

Granted, many college-educated women find tremendous fulfillment in their professions, and those who have truly chosen that path after an honest assessment of the alternatives and their likely fitness as a parent should be applauded. No one is hoping for more inadequate mothers. But so many have been deluded into thinking they would find fulfillment down a career path, and it doesn't turn out that way. These women will never know if turning their priorities around—putting family first and work second—might have given them the life they always wanted. Some of the most grief-stricken are not only single and barren but also carrying the burden of knowing they murdered their legacy by having abortions because they bought the Leftist lie of reproductive choice.

SLAUGHTER OF INNOCENTS

Why is the Left so adamant about abortion rights? Why do they insist on tax-funded abortions for the poor? Is the argument really about the woman's choice or the elite's choice? No public medical research, media survey, or national study has been conducted to measure the emotional damage of post-abortive women, but a growing body of evidence suggests that a high percentage, as high as 90 percent, of women who have an abortion suffer emotional and psychiatric stress, including as many as 10 percent requiring psychiatric hospitalization or other professional treatment. As many as 30,000 women each year suffer emotional trauma severe enough to render them unable to work. And women who have had abortions are nine times more likely to commit suicide than those who haven't. Over 200,000 women who have had abortions in America have joined post-abortion support groups such as Women Exploited by Abortion, Victims of Choice, and American Victims of Abortion. But as Dr. David C. Reardon notes in *Aborted Women: Silent No More*, this number only includes those willing to admit they have been hurt by abortion. Many others may be suffering in humiliated silence.

Some data, however, is more useful in decrypting the motives of the Left. One study out of the University of Chicago boasted that abortion has had a positive effect on society in that potential criminals were being killed off. As Steven Levitt noted in the August 8, 1999, *Chicago Tribune*, this conclusion was based on the fact that abortion industry giants such as Planned Parenthood deliberately targeted inner city neighborhoods and indigent communities.

With seventeen years of pro-life activism under my belt, I wonder to which poverty group will society eventually assign these women who believed the feminist lie that their unborn were simply a matter of choice. I have counseled numerous women dealing with post-abortion emotions. Some are suicidal. Some are mental basket cases. Some are loveless zombies no longer able to connect in any relationship. One woman in particular is still deep in mourning twenty years later.

We can hope the data slowly being gathered is ultimately compelling to future scholars, politicians, and media commentators. Although it is folly for the hope of the poor to rest with a society driven to simply bandage pain or make hard choices easier, it is likely new state-run welfare programs will be proposed. The best way to help someone in a moral dilemma is to first help him or her understand that they are in a moral dilemma. There are two main reasons feminists can reject what science has proven in the last twenty years with regards to killing an unborn child. First, they've abandoned any belief in absolute, transcendent truth, so God is irrelevant in their minds. Second, they've denied there are obvious fundamental and natural differences that God has created in men and women. Pregnancy makes it obvious that these differences are real. Therefore, the ultimate vision of the sexual liberationist is to make pregnancy voluntary.

Planned Pregnancy

The secret behind this "make pregnancy voluntary" movement was that abortion disproportionately targeted minorities and the poor. Many Americans are unaware that Planned Parenthood founder Margaret Sanger aligned herself with eugenicists. The eugenicist movement in the early twentieth century strongly espoused racial supremacy and purity of the white race. Wanting to purify bloodlines, eugenicists encouraged the fit to reproduce and the unfit to restrict their reproduction. They sought to contain the "inferior" races through segregation, sterilization, birth control, and abortion.

Sanger began with contraception and sterilization. Her writing and lectures were based on her belief that birth control in the lower classes was a way to "breed out the scourges of transmissible disease, mental defect, poverty, lawlessness, and crime. . . since these classes would be decreasing in number instead of breeding like weeds," as she noted in the *Birth Control Review*, May 1919. One of Sanger's *Birth Control Review* essays was entitled "We Must Breed a Race of Thoroughbreds" (November 1921). An excerpt from a 1923 lecture—cited in David Kennedy's *Birth Control in America: The Career of Margaret Sanger*—is most illuminating:

> It now remains for the U.S. government to set a sensible example to the world by offering a bonus or yearly pension to all obviously unfit parents who allow themselves to be sterilized by harmless and scientific means. In this way the moron and the diseased would have no posterity to inherit their unhappy condition. The number of the feeble-minded would decrease and a heavy burden would be lifted from the shoulders of the fit.

Sanger recruited Fisk University's first president, Dr. Charles S. Johnson, prominent Harlem, New York, minister, Dr. Adam Clayton Powell Sr., and black author and sociologist, Dr. W.E.B. DuBois (ironic when you consider the feminists mentioned earlier who wanted to tear down the W.E.B. DuBois library), to support her cause. Sanger was often invited to speak at Dr. Powell's church about how birth control would improve the status of blacks, and DuBois, credited as one of the founders of the NAACP, called for a "more liberal attitude" among black churches.

DuBois pointed to the "inevitable clash of ideals between those Negroes who were striving to improve their economic position and those whose religious faith made the limitation of children a sin." He criticized the "mass ignorant Negroes" who bred "carelessly and disastrously" so that the increase among blacks was from the part of the population "least intelligent and fit" and "least able to rear their children properly." Dr. Juluette Bartlett Pack documents this sad display from so prominent a black leader in her essay, "A Historical View of Eugenics and Its Role in Abortion in Black America," for AbortionFacts.com. DuBois's statements are the intellectual precursors to Surgeon General Jocelyn Elders's frightening decree ("every child a planned and wanted child") during the Clinton Era. No one bothered asking what happens to the unwanted child because the answer was too barbaric—dismemberment and disposal.

Sanger's ideas have been allowed to permeate the black community, paving the way to their future with blood in the name of reproductive rights. Today, Planned Parenthood is the number one provider of abortion against African-Americans. Dr. George Grant, a prolific author on Planned Parenthood's genocidal ambitions, observed in his book *Grand Illusions*, "During the 1980s when Planned Parenthood shifted its focus from community-based clinics to school-based clinics, it again targeted inner-city minority neighborhoods." He points out that of the more than one hundred school-based clinics that opened nationwide in the eighties, none were located at predominately white schools, and none were at suburban middle-class schools. All were in black, minority, or ethnic schools.

Effect on Blacks

Interestingly, Rev. Jesse Jackson was opposed to abortion until his Democratic presidential bid in 1984. He too used to state that it was genocide, but not anymore. In fact, Jackson, along with most current black leaders, supports all forms and procedures of abortion from the moment of conception throughout the ninth month. When the Congress took up debates on what is commonly called "partial birth" abortion, only two of the thirty-eight Congressional Black Caucus members voted against banning the procedure. Many of the arguments used to defend partial birth abortion were so similar to those used to support slavery that voting in favor of a ban would seem to be a no-brainer for blacks. But the extreme abortion rights activists had the Democratic party by the short hairs, and the Black Caucus members couldn't muster the backbone to break ranks.

Proponents of slavery argued that the motive behind the Missouri Compromise of 1820, which declared new territory as "free" was really an incremental step to end all slavery. Liberals used that same argument to support partial birth abortion by stating that the vote really isn't about one procedure. It's about getting a foothold to roll back abortion law broadly. The *Dred Scott* Supreme Court decision allowed slave masters freedom from government intervention regarding the treatment of slaves because it concluded that the slave was the "property" of the owner. Senator Dianne Feinstein used that same argument when she presupposed that the unborn fetus is the property of the woman stating that the decision for partial birth abortion "is between a woman and her doctor."

Although most Americans have tried to ignore or have grown comfortable with an average of 5,000 human deaths *per day* at the hands of abortionists, according to Alan Guttmacher Institute statistics, our cultural conscience is not completely calloused. Efforts to show video of the horrendous procedure of partial-birth abortion are consistently blocked by liberals, precisely because they know that the outrage of such grotesque images reveals the slaughter as the crime that it is and makes the argument of reproductive choice patently absurd, much like calling Hitler's murdering millions of Jews "ethnic cleansing." Just cleaning up the gene pool; really, what's all the fuss? The real irony is that black leaders, who use slavery statistics that bring attention to the terrible slaughter of millions of black slaves while still at sea, would blindly or cynically support a process which accounts for hundreds of thousands of black deaths each year. According to Rev. Johnny Hunter, president of Life Education and Resource Network (LEARN), a national pro-life organization tracking abortion and blacks, 34.7 percent of the 1.3 million abortions performed in America in 2000 were performed on black women—that's 452,000 black Americans murdered annually, with the whole-hearted support of these same black leaders. Let us hear no more patronizing nonsense about reparations from these hypocrites who support the slaughter of their own people.

While today's civil rights leaders dare to suggest they speak for the rights of the poor and underprivileged, few support alternatives to abortion. LEARN documents that African-American abortion rates are running two-to-one against live births, which means approximately 1,452 deaths every day. Since 1973, there have been thirteen million blacks killed by abortion. By ignoring the racial impact of abortion on blacks, these black leaders affirm that their leftist support of radical feminism is more important to them than progress for the black poor. If Harriet Tubman or Sojourner Truth were alive today, you would likely find them picketing in front of Planned Parenthoods clinics, allies of the annual Say So March and LEARN, and forcefully coming to the rescue of young women like Natalyn.

Natalyn was fifteen years old and pregnant. The nurse at her public high school in Los Angeles gave her a bus token to ride the city bus to a local abortion clinic. At the clinic Natalyn found out she was six months pregnant and an abortion at this stage would require a three-day procedure called Laminaria. This is where they induce dilation prior to inducing labor. On the third day of the abortion procedure, the baby is poisoned in the womb and delivered dead. The second day of the procedure, Natalyn's friend called me because she could hear Natalyn screaming in the back room of the abortion clinic. Retrieving the girls from the clinic required that they pretend to be hitchhikers, because if I went into the clinic to retrieve students I would be violating the law. According to California law, since they were school age and it was during school hours and the school nurse was involved, the girls were deemed school property. "School property?" I asked. "I thought the Fourteenth Amendment prevented us from regarding people as property." Apparently not. The school nurse could send a student to an abortion clinic without parental consent, but I needed consent to take Natalyn to the hospital in order to help her save the baby she now wanted. Abortion on demand is our modern Roman wall, where babies can be left to die, and the government makes it a crime to intervene.

OUT-OF-WEDLOCK BIRTHS

Choice. The operative word of the pro-abortion movement, coupled with welfare programs, opened the door for out-of-wedlock birth rates to soar. If the "right" to have children has nothing to do with marital status but everything to do with "choice" how does a society manage the indigent who choose not to marry yet have multiple children by a variety of sexual partners?

Choice. If it is legal and even in vogue to act upon any or all sexual preferences, how can the government stand against the rising tide of sexually transmitted disease, divorce, and child abandonment?

Choice. This is where the rubber meets the road in Uncle Sam's attack against marriage. We would hope that under a growing awareness of the impact of feminism most women would choose not to become unpaid whores. We don't want anyone to experience abortion. We hope no one grows old and dies alone. But how do you tell poor women to ignore the new rules of sexual freedom when they have no social or moral reference point?

The War on Poverty was intended to rid the nation of child poverty. Only the erosion of marriage and the growth of single-parent families can explain the lack of progress. According to researcher Robert Rector of the Heritage Foundation, in 2002 the poverty rate for all children in married couple families was 8.2 percent compared to the poverty rate for all children in single-parent families, which was four times higher at 35.2 percent. Nearly a third of all American children born last year were born out of wedlock. The African-American out-of-wedlock birth rate is consistently around 70 percent, according to figures from the U.S. Department of Health and Human Services and the Census Bureau.

It is generally accepted that family collapse is the root cause of many social problems including poverty, crime, drug abuse, and school failure. Children born in single-parent households are seven times more likely to be poor than those born to couples who stay married. Girls raised in welfare homes are five times more likely to give birth before marriage. Boys from inner-city homes are twice as likely to engage in crime. Is it unreasonable to suggest that the feminist revolution against marriage severely damaged the social viability of disadvantaged children?

With the help of feminism, marriage in secular America is dying. In 1965, about 11 percent of all families with children were single-parent households. In 1995, that number was dangerously close to one in three American families. Research by CURE found that, of those homes, about 90 percent are homes without a father.

In his book *Fatherless America*, David Blankenhorn explains that, by the time they are teenagers, half of America's children will live without a father in the home. Never before has our nation faced such a plague of absentee fathers. We talk about this issue, get upset about it—divorce, youth violence, domestic violence, the weakening of parental authority—but no one wants to make the obvious connection to the common cause for all of these social problems: the willingness of men to flee from their children's lives.

Now that dear Mister Rogers has left us, we need to tell our children more than ever that they are valuable, that life is valuable. Marriage between a man and a woman, in the sight of God, affirmed before the public, and honored until death, is an honorable choice which even hardcore atheists should support, because it is society's first and best chance at survival.

Reproductive choice is no more defensible than ethnic cleansing, and our society and morality are severely weakened when we embrace it. The impoverished women having out-of-wedlock children have been convinced by feminists to not even consider marriage.

Forty years of Democrat-controlled government has given these women the infrastructure to be sexually active without facing reproductive consequences. The Left believes it is actually helping them, but it is destroying the family and the primary hope for these women to escape poverty.

SOCIAL PREDATORS

And what of men? Freed from the responsibility of family by Uncle Sam, there is little to hold them to the home and much to pull them away.

America barely blushed when former basketball player "Magic" Johnson said that, by age twenty-five, he had had hundreds of sexual partners. It wasn't necessary for him to recall their names because, unlike syphilis, an HIV diagnosis did not require tracking. Besides, he's wealthy, able to help fund AIDS research and purchase his own supply of life-sustaining medicine until science comes up with a cure. Much more inquiry was made when Wilt Chamberlain proclaimed in his book that he had over ten thousand sexual conquests. Testosterone surged as men attempted to imagine the possibilities with envy.

How is it that black leaders neglect the impact of negative assessments of marriage and religious morality on men? Most inner city men are the epitome of moral values gone astray. The facts are clear: Boys without married fathers are more likely to grow up to become men without a moral compass, and without a moral compass guys are woefully ill-equipped to temper their sexual urges.

The central issue is neither racism nor poverty but faith and ethics. Unless a poor man adopts a value system that is consistent with freedom and personal responsibility, all of the capitalist moralizing about pulling himself up by his boot straps will not motivate him. He doesn't care. If success is equated to the acquisition of things, if money is the motivator, then engineering a short cut is brilliance. His attitude is all about expediency—get what you can when you can. A variety of women are his due, a variety of babies merely a byproduct of getting what he wants. All of the racial politics for more welfare programs will not motivate him. He doesn't care about the impact of his actions on his community or the women he uses and damages.

Bill Clinton legitimized the behavior of the sexual predator when he convinced the majority of Americans that his adulterous sex acts in the Oval Office were simply a private affair. Nationally acclaimed black author Toni Morrison affirmed him by exalting him as "America's first black president." Considering the predatory behavior of the average low-income black male, this designation is certainly deserved.

Clinton's qualifications? He came from a broken and abusive household, wore it as a badge of honor, and pretended that it was normal and that it had no affect on his psyche, current behavior, or accomplishments. All of the members of the Congressional Black Caucus defended him during his impeachment and went to bat for him on the media talk shows. Hillary endorsed his choices as well. She said that the attack against him was a "radical right wing conspiracy." Her unintentional message to women: "As long as you have position and influence, it doesn't matter what the man that fathers your children does. Put up with it. Enable him. It's all about money and power."

Now, while most communities can sift through this kind of sociopolitical outrage relatively unscathed because of the resilience of their traditional culture, blacks in America have a patchwork culture—the legacy of slavery—and tend to be blown about by every liberal wind of doctrine, swallowing Leftist lies without complaint because the psychology of blame appeals to them. Liberals assert that religion is what caused slavery, leaving the black underclass to instead adopt its values from a pop culture that predisposes ghetto girls to live off Uncle Sam's plantation and gangsta guys to slide into their natural state of social predator living only for the moment.

In *The Unheavenly City Revisited,* political scientist Edward C. Banfield describes the crisis this way:

At the present-oriented end of the scale, the lower-class individual lives from moment to moment. If he has any awareness of a future, it is of something fixed, fated, beyond his control: things happen to him, he does not make them happen. Impulse governs his behavior, either because he cannot discipline himself to sacrifice a present for a future satisfaction or because he has no sense of the future. He is therefore radically improvident: whatever he cannot use immediately he considers valueless.

Banfield goes on to say that the male need for sexual gratification and personal adventure overrides all other impulses, making it impossible to stick with a steady job. He does only what is necessary to survive, bouncing from job to job with no satisfaction in his work.

Your average lower class person has lousy self-esteem and not much sense of who he is. He is likely to labor under feelings of depression or despondency. While being aggressive or suspicious, he is also likely to be enslaved to one form of dependency or another. Unable to sustain any ongoing relationship with the opposite sex, he is unlikely to get married. Without any feelings of connection to his community or fellow citizens, he loathes authority and is likely to feel he has been forced into his situation and wants to take revenge. He joins no organizations and has no actual interest in politics. He will not vote unless someone pays him to do it.

In *The Millionaire Next Door* by Thomas J. Stanley, Ph.D., and William D. Danko, Ph.D., we find a picture at the other end of the spectrum. In that book, the authors concluded that the major common denominator among the wealthy is a sense of purpose and character. The message of most liberals, however, is that the wealthy are exploitive thieves because they push other people into poverty for

118

their own gain. In the liberal view, this means redistribution of their wealth is an appropriate moral vengeance against their lust and greed.

To be a person of character as defined by the liberal, one must embrace their panacea of equal rights and pluralism. Their insistence for religious relativism tills the fallow ground of political absolutism. The only time character enters into the discussion is when those who are productive are not willing to turn over more of their income to Uncle Sam for support of the unproductive and their offspring. Then the demonizing begins, for only a fat cat racist would refuse to help the downtrodden, especially when the fat cat racist created the whole problem in the first place!

NO WORK, ALL PLAY

When character is on a slow but slippery downward slope, you can easily tell how this moral relativism has impacted the person's behavior by listening to what people say about him when he's not around. Take the average poor, black male, for example:

Grandma:	"He ain't here, officer, is there something I can do for you?"
Mom:	"Work, no he ain't at work! That boy ain't had no job since I raised him."
Foster Mom:	"What has he done this time?"
First Baby's Mama:	"That nigga betta not be at that bitch's house else I'ma kill 'em."
Pregnant Girlfriend:	"If he don't git that nappy head out my bed and go git a job I'ma call his mama."
New Girlfriend:	"Last I saw him he was on the corner with his homies."

Just an average day eavesdropping at any one of the 3,000 housing projects where Uncle Sam tucks his dependents while their leaders are out demanding that blacks need reparations, affirmative action, and a higher welfare check.

Do you remember the ex-boyfriend I talked about that had all of his belongings in a shopping cart? He had a classic case of lack of character that Uncle Sam could not engineer. Drew grew up in Florida as the only child of a single mother. His father was not to be found. Drew is one of several men I have met over the years that have never met nor seen their fathers. One, now thirty-eight, confided that he still gets anxious on every street corner and at every social gathering because the stranger next to him "could be my dad."

Drew was tall, poised, smooth-talking, and very handsome even as a boy. His mom's friends spoiled him. His mom smothered him. She was a professional woman and offered him lots of goodies throughout his adolescent years. But Drew learned to like the goodies the girls offered him better. They would do his homework, pay his way to the movies, buy him clothes, and gratify his sexual desires.

After bombing out of college due to the low-test scores that put his basketball scholarship at risk, Drew moved to California. I met him within a year of that transition. He was living with a friend and was working full-time as a tentmaker. He loved having a variety of women, but it didn't bother me. My sexual lifestyle was in line with the sexual revolution as well. Besides, he was the only guy I knew that had a real job, an appealing factor when he suggested that we shack up after his roommate had also moved a girlfriend into their one bedroom apartment.

We never discussed marriage. It was the 1980s. Marriage was an outdated concept that kids of the seventies had been conditioned to not bring up. Our high schools had said that it was a moral judgment not to be imposed on others. When he got me pregnant, I had an abortion. It just seemed like the right thing to do. After all, which of us was to adjust our lifestyle around the responsibility of providing for a kid?

Our life together would be free of all entanglements. Our apartment was the all night hang out for all of our homeless, sex-crazed, or druggie friends. Little did I know that his commitment to work was no deeper than his commitment to me. His full-time employment lasted little more than six months before he got a new job as the supplier of the neighborhood weed. Before long, he was pushing a lot more than marijuana, the crack heads were starting to hang around, and every night I wondered when the cops would bust in.

Two years later I got pregnant by someone else and moved on. Years later when I saw him with the shopping cart, I almost didn't recognize him because that lifestyle had taken its toll; the drugs had so distorted his once flawless face and dreamy eyes. He didn't recognize me but wanted to know if I could spare some change.

What happened? Did government not do enough to integrate his schools? Couldn't the affirmative action program at his college spare him from flunking out? Shouldn't his employer have been able to drug test? Could an absolute moral code have saved him? An affirmative to the last question would present a far better bet than trusting Uncle Sam or his enablers in the black leadership.

The great mission of the Rainbow/PUSH Coalition, the Urban League, and the NAACP is to alleviate racism and, by golly, they will not be distracted by the fact that the people they say they represent are locked in moral freefall.

The Left has an excuse for every problem created by their value-free welfare ideology. The disproportionate number of African-Americans who are illiterate is the fault of Republicans for not adequately funding education. The disproportionate number of African-Americans on welfare is the fault of Republicans for not supporting federal mandates for a livable wage. Greedy capitalists who refuse to locate their businesses in the inner cities cause high unemployment in the black community. Black crime is the result of a racist judicial system. Black drug addiction is the result of disenfranchisement because white people won't redistribute more of their wealth to help the under-privileged. Besides, as Congresswoman Maxine Waters pointed out, the CIA deliberately pumped drugs into the black community to destroy it. The filthy living conditions, the graffiti, the barred-up stores, the garbage-littered streets—all the fault of Republicans.

Taxpayers vent their frustration on talk radio. College kids protest for "social justice." Fourteen-year-old girls get pregnant. Nine-year-old boys get guns. Democrats cry for more domestic aid. Republicans tout a faith-based initiative that promises to entangle a well-meaning Church in the welfare disaster.

Banfield notes that, "So long as the city contains a sizable lower class, nothing can be done about its most serious problems. Good jobs may be offered to all, but some will remain chronically unemployed. Slums may be demolished, but if the housing that replaces them is occu-pied by the lower class it will shortly be turned into new slums." He goes on to say that welfare payments could be increased to levels two or three times what is normal, and people would still live in awful con-ditions. You can add more teachers and better schools, but the children who come from morally broken homes will turn the school into a black-board jungle. And whether they graduate or drop out, they will still be functionally illiterate and unable to function as a productive member of society. You can fill the streets with policeman, and you will still have high crime rates and civil disruption.

Why?

Because Bill Clinton is wrong. It's not *just* the economy, stupid! A thriving economy is not the solution. Although the poor need free enterprise, capital investment, and rising productivity in order to attain better living standards, the lack of a sustainable moral code and value system brings such endeavors to naught.

Rev. Jesse Jackson is wrong. Although America still has a long road to travel towards racial neutrality, the promotion of moral relativism amongst the poor exacerbates the welfare state.

Al Sharpton is wrong. It is impossible to pluck the splinter from the white man's eye when blinded by the beam in your own eye.

Hillary Clinton is wrong. The government should only do for others what they are not capable of doing for themselves. As George Gilder points out in his book *Men and Marriage*, "The breakdown of monogamy produces unproductive and disruptive men."

The answer is not a jobs program. The creation of jobs will not remedy the pathology of males freed from sexual socialization. "Help Wanted" signs can be everywhere in a city, but when the attitude of uncommitted males is rebellion against work, they will not even show up for an interview.

Gilder explains this rejection of established society in this way:

> Jobs alone have never sufficed to break through the single male bias for street life, the peer-group pursuit of short-term excitements, the easy money of petty crime, and the easy women who succumb to the rhythms of young men. Entry-level jobs are unpleasant, often less appealing at first than the swashbuckling life as a "free-lance," hanging out and raising hell with males and freeloading off welfare women.

According to Gilder, men will not readily accept the ongoing strictures of the role of provider unless they feel compelled to do so. "During the last twenty years, middle-class blacks acquired a net 4 million skilled jobs, getting new skilled work at a pace between three and five times as fast as whites, while the millions of unskilled jobs opening up were resolutely shunned by poor blacks." Thus, the daily routine of unproductive and disruptive men is to "kick it," watch some TV, get high, or "get some" on a conjugal visit with his baby's mama. "The social relationship of the community no longer revolved around the male as leading provider and the female as procreator, ultimately joining in monogamous love and marriage. Rather the woman is both provider and procreator, and the man and woman join only in male-oriented copulation that leads nowhere—except on occasion to an illegitimate child," Gilder concludes.

I've seen how that game is played because it is very popular in the hood. The predator stops by at the first and the fifteenth of the month when the welfare check arrives. He goes back to his homeboys sexually satisfied and with a little money in his pocket. She finds out a month or two later that she's pregnant again. He gets busted for another violation. What is the biggest complaint from his so-called leaders about this scenario? Three strikes. "Them crackers can't wait to lock a brother up," is the buzz behind closed doors. In front of the media, the same sentiment is dressed in political terms.

"The [U.S. Supreme] Court's right wing majority got it wrong again, ruling that these obscene sentences do not violate the Eighth Amendment's ban on cruel and unusual punishment," argued Rev. Jesse Jackson, president of the Rainbow/PUSH Coalition, in his March 9, 2003, Tribune Media column. "Somehow the justices did not find 25 years in prison 'grossly disproportionate' to the crime of shoplifting." So what if two felony crimes precede the third strike?

I tried to explain to several African-American groups that the offenders were extended mercy twice and they made the choice to violate another man's property at the risk of their personal freedom. No, according to their leaders, the white man's conspiracy against them was the motivator, and incredibly, most believed that lie.

"The court was blinded not only to elemental justices, but to common sense as well," Jackson continued. "Across the country, these absurd laws have tied the hands of judges, and forced long sentences for literally hundreds of thousands of inmates for nonviolent crimes. With racial profiling by police, entrenched prosecutorial bias, and often stacked juries, the victims of these injustices are overwhelmingly minorities—African American and Latino—and male." But Jackson takes his cause one step further to enshrine the shiftlessness and laziness of these societal delinquents. In his protest against the Three Strikes Law, Jackson brings up the subject of inmate labor crews. "They pick up litter, cut grass, do landscaping, haul trash, and even do carpeting and painting."

The problem here? Said Jackson,

> With more young black men in prison than in college, the US has discovered the closest thing to slave labor since, well, slavery. Profile them, track them down, lock them up with extreme sentences, and then put them to work for eight dollars a day. No wonder George Bush says he doesn't believe in a minimum wage, much less in raising it. Not when you can get disciplined workers at eight dollars a day.
>
> George Bush offers the Turks $26 billion in grants and loans to loan us their bases so our troops can defend them, but he offers nothing in his budget to help the cities and states in their budget crisis. Prisons and schools will be more overcrowded, with fewer services and less adult supervision. Since poor schools will suffer the most, more children will drop out or fail—providing even more fodder for the prisons.

There are three things I want to point out in this predictable and inflammatory statement from the Rev. Jackson. First, his statement that there are more young black men in prison than in college is misleading. As the saying goes, repeat a lie enough times and it becomes a destructive firestorm that people believe is true.

According to the U.S. Census Bureau, in 2000 there were just over two million male prisoners in the United States. Blacks make up 40 percent of that number, which means that there are 791,600 black men in prison. That number represents about 7 percent of the entire black male population of 16.5 million. According to the U.S. Department of

Education, 25 percent of black males between 18 and 24 are enrolled in college. There are 1.8 million black males between 18 and 24 of which 603,032 are in college. While it is true that the number of black males in college is lower than the number of total black males in prison, in order for Jackson's premise to be accurate, 75 percent of the black males in prison must be of college age, which they are not. Although black prison rates are disproportionately high, as usual Jackson is trying to make the picture more ugly than it is. He wants to make the discrepancy racial when in fact it is moral.

When blacks play by the moral rulebook, get married, and work hard, they tend to prosper and are in no need of Jackson's shakedown artistry.

According to Claudette Bennett, chief of the racial statistics branch of the Census Bureau, black married couples do well. "More than half of all black married families had incomes of $50,000 or more," she said in a recent report. The report showed, "In education, black achievement is at a record level: 79 percent have at least a high school degree (up four percentage points from the 1997 report) and 17 percent have at least a bachelor's degree (up four percentage points)." It also showed that among black couples 26.9 percent make $75,000 or more and more than 48 percent of blacks owned their homes in 2002.

When was the last time Jackson touted these remarkable accomplishments or compared the six million blacks in military uniform with the blacks in prison? Ah, but that would defeat his agenda to undermine defense spending for more education spending.

Second, Jackson dismisses the value of work to the inmates by equating it to slavery. Is it better to cage the criminal like an animal than to have him labor productively? The criminal owes a debt to society, and productivity helps him pay that debt. And just as important, productivity helps the criminal. The personal satisfaction one derives from laboring should not be underestimated during debates about putting prisoners to work. Work is good for the mind, body, and soul of any person who provides a service, fulfills a duty, or completes a task. When H.L. Mencken criticized the soul-stifling cruelty of prison, the reason was that the men led boring, nonproductive lives. Liberals like Jackson believe that it is better to let the victims of theft and thuggery live with their losses while supporting their attackers in tax-financed penitentiaries. Better to pen up the criminals with murderers and molestors, color televisions, weight rooms, and basketball courts than have him build a work résumé.

Third, Jackson blames the school drop-out and failure rates of poor kids on state budget crises. With community libraries and the Internet, this excuse is so nineteenth century.

OFF THE HOOK

Social order and maturity into manhood does not come naturally for boys. It must be taught. Girls are an easy study. You don't have to tell a girl that she is becoming an adult. Her body tells her at puberty that womanhood is preparation for motherhood. Her natural instinct is rooted in a reproductive cycle that has built-in patterns to govern her sexuality. That is why motherhood comes so naturally for the majority of women and why nurturing is so easy. Boys, on the other hand, learn at puberty that their bodies respond sexually to a wide range of stimuli. Boys must be taught the responsibilities of an adult because their natural instinct is to play the field, to sexually be on the prowl. The blatant display of public homosexuality highlights this fact of human nature. The culture of a society and its women are the social forces necessary to restrain the male instinct, allowing men to be productive, rather than *re*productive (or destructive) members of society.

The welfare state undermines this teaching. It provides men an exit from marriage, which is already suffering from the onslaughts of feminism, and thus frees them to tomcat around instead of building and nurturing stable families. Thus what is otherwise a place where boys can be socialized, taught a work ethic, and raised to achieve—namely the family—simply disappears, and America, especially those in the lower class, are the poorer for it.

6

Uncle Sam's Children

Back in 1965, Daniel Patrick Moynihan related the social and economic problems of blacks in America to the disintegration of the black family. Most of his political colleagues then thought that ending racial discrimination could solve the problems of black poverty. As assistant secretary of labor, Moynihan published a paper report called *The Negro Family: The Case for National Action*, which rocked social thinkers everywhere. His concern was that while black unemployment was decreasing, the number of blacks on welfare was increasing. His paper suggested black poverty was not just economic or legal but had a great deal to do with the breakdown of the Negro family. Moynihan's conclusions were feverishly attacked for "blaming the victim" and readily dismissed.

Things have only worsened since the 1960s. When Moynihan first identified the collapse of the black family as a problem, there was only one point of contention—whether his hypothesis was true. It has been proven to be manifestly true in the years since. When Moynihan wrote, one out of every four black babies were born to unmarried women. Over the next forty years, the number of black children born to unmarried women has almost tripled.

And to further complicate the situation, as these problems have worsened so has the culture in which they must be addressed. Here in 2003 (and for the foreseeable future), this debate revolves around more fundamental questions, such as whether family should matter at all and whether our traditional notions of a husband and wife raising their children have any relevance. In other words, we're losing ground.

We can argue until doomsday about how the damage was done, but the indisputable fact remains: today the black family as an institution lies nearly in ruins. This is tragic because values are transmitted through family, which means much of the black community has lost the core delivery system for values. Like children in any dysfunctional family, black children learn from what they observe. With so many children born outside of marriage, in families with no father present, core values are missing from daily life, and children are forced to look outside to popular culture for guidance.

Without the help of religious instruction, the illegitimate child learns from television, movies, the press, their politicians, and their sports heroes that you get ahead by having more money and more power and that being free means any consensual lifestyle is acceptable. They learn that ascribing categories of "right" and "wrong" to behavior is a violation of their rights. Worse, they learn that promiscuous sexual behavior is normal and acceptable, leading them toward activities that endanger their lives and perpetuate the cycle.

Deliberate or not, the indoctrination of these children is quite successful and difficult to reverse if allowed to run its course unchecked. Deprived of hope and any sense of meaning or social responsibility, they live essentially as animals—hunting in packs, watching their backs, and seeking only the pleasure or need of the moment.

Historian Paul Johnson focused the issue in a question posed in his seminal book, *A History of the American People*: "Can ideals and altruism—the desire to build the perfect community—be mixed successfully with acquisitiveness and ambition, without which no dynamic society can be built at all?" The answer of course is, yes, they can be mixed success-fully. Acquisitiveness tempered by altruism is enlightened self-interest, which says, I have a strong desire to help people and a strong desire to make a million dollars. These goals are not necessarily mutually exclu-sive.

Sadly, the popular culture that becomes the ideological mother's milk of illegitimate children is devoid of ideals and altruism, leaving only acquisitive ambition. Small wonder they lead lives of quiet or vio-lent desperation and have little patience to sit in school. If the whole point of education is to improve your ability to acquire things, there are simpler methods, like drug-dealing, theft, and prostitution. These meth-ods are not legal, but after all, from a certain perspective, prison is just a more radical form of welfare—either way they win. (Given the right spin, it can also appear as a peculiar form of status—hence the prison-styled clothing designs made popular in America's inner cities. Being persecuted by "The Man" is seen as cool, and wearing emblems of this persecution is too.)

The passions of adolescence surging through kids with no moral compass are frightening. Only the worst kind of wishful thinking would allow us to expect anything other than promiscuity when such behav-ior is communicated and sanctioned over and over in the media they consume every day.

This fact does not support the case for the victimization of blacks, nor does it offer new excuses for blacks to abrogate responsibility for their lives. However, it is crucial for all Americans to be aware of what we are doing with our precious freedom and the price that is being paid in the most vulnerable parts of our society. Black reality is, in a way, a mirror image reflecting back on America, and, in this sense, we are paying for the sins of our fathers. The very fact that Americans tol-erate taxes to support countless illegitimate children rather than iden-tify and deal with root causes is proof that our priorities are in desperate need of realignment. The pulsating primitive rhythms and rhymes of rap music simply reflect the truths that are transmitted to blacks through the wafer-thin veneer of popular American culture. With all the subtlety of a sledgehammer, our youth are bludgeoned with the message that life is all about money, power, and sex. Illegitimacy, youth crime, and illiteracy rates make it abundantly clear that our children are getting the message.

FATHERLESS BOYS

Less than 150 years ago the majority of blacks in America were slaves. Less than fifty years ago the ancestors of these slaves were subjected to discriminatory laws and aggressive racial segregation. Today, however, their descendents generate and circulate a half trillion dollars annually; 70 percent live above the poverty line; 60 percent own stocks; and 49 percent live in suburban neighborhoods, according to the U.S. Census Bureau and research by the National Center for Policy Analysis. Where family life is strong, black life in America is successful. So why do liberal leaders today ignore the growing trend of black family breakdown? Why do they concentrate all of their efforts on protecting the very social programs that have evidently contributed to the major problem confronting African-Americans today?

Children born into unmarried households are more likely to succumb to peer pressure, experiment with tobacco or drugs, become involved in adolescent sexual activities, be a victim of domestic violence and/or sexual abuse, and perform poorly in or drop out of school. Trying to rear children outside of marriage is a tough challenge. Figures from the Department of Health and Human Services show that single black mothers head 43 percent of all black families, and among black single mothers about six in ten make less than $25,000 annually. The problem is not a race issue or poverty issue as most black leaders want America to think. About four in ten single white women also make less than $25,000 annually. According to a compilation of figures from the Population Resource Bureau and AmeriStat, some 80 percent of all children admitted to psychiatric hospitals are from single-parent homes. But liberals are stuck in the economic and legal game plan of the sixties, unable to explain why—after forty years of liberal social engineering—Uncle Sam's children are still at risk.

The first place a child learns about boundaries is from his or her parents, and without specific boundaries children don't know how to function. Remember, values are transmitted through family, and the black community has substantially lost this core delivery system. Boys learn how to treat girls by seeing how their father treats their mother. Girls learn how to treat boys by seeing how their mother treats their father. This is not rocket science. When the father is not married to the mother the first lesson the child learns is that commitment is not an important value. Disengagement from commitment is a form of abandonment that drives children from single-parent households into a desperate search to find meaning or a sense of belonging from their peers. This means more girls with babies and more boys in gangs.

Since Moynihan first questioned welfare policies in the sixties, the rate of births to unmarried teenagers has nearly doubled. Teen mothers accounted for about 30 percent of all unwed births in 1996. Half go on welfare within one year of the birth of their first child, and 77 percent are on welfare within five years of the child's birth, according to research done by CURE in 1997. Many out-of-wedlock births involve mothers who had their first child as an unmarried teen. Most black leaders don't seem to care that Uncle Sam makes illegitimacy easy by providing shelter, food, medical assistance, childcare, and a little cash for these girls who produce children before marriage. In fact, the Congressional Black Caucus, NAACP, and other "traditional" civil rights organizations adamantly opposed welfare reform.

Julie Grace reminded us in her 1994 *Time* magazine article, "There Are No Children Here," of the story of Robert "Yummy" Sandifer. Robert was taken by fellow gang members under a Chicago expressway and was shot twice in the skull. He was eleven years old. Burned with cigarettes and beaten as a baby, Robert was only three when first called to the attention of child welfare authorities. His first encounter with the judicial system was at age eight when he was arrested for shoplifting. His formative years were not spent playing catch with his dad in the backyard. He was bounced from group homes and detention centers due to recurring arrests on twenty-three different charges. Finally, Robert tried to impress local gang members by spraying gunfire into a group of children on a playground. A fourteen-year-old girl was killed. When his own gang members feared he would talk to the police in exchange for leniency, they shot him.

More than two million juveniles are arrested in the United States each year, the majority because of gang-related activities. In California, 40 percent of youth in custody have a parent who has done time. Homicide is the second leading cause of death among all 15- to 24-year-olds and is now the third leading cause of death among elementary school children, ages 5 to 14. The death rate by homicide in the 1980s of youth between the ages of 15 and 19 increased by 60 percent. For African-American males the homicide rate is almost eight times that of the rate of whites. Between 1986 and 1992 alone, the number of children killed by firearms jumped 144 percent. As was already mentioned, going to jail for most gang members is seen as a glamorous rite of passage that earns respect and status. According to the Department of Justice, the rate of known homicide offenders ages 14 to 17 climbed from 16.2 per 100,000 in 1990 to 19.1 per 100,000 in 1994.

Despite these facts, the public outcry from the black elite is over racial profiling and minimum/maximum sentences for perpetual criminals, rather than the problem that these boys are raised in fatherless homes. More was said recently to disparage the brave black military men going to war than about the self-destructive tendencies poor black males suffer from because their parents don't stay together.

ADOLESCENT SEX

Uncle Sam developed a new program to bandage the growing problems of teenage births. The program is called Title X, which became law in 1970 and grew to a $200 million program by 1995. It provides sex education to prevent pregnancies, abortion to prevent births, and special accommodations for the teenage mother at her public school. Advocates and supporters of Title X thought mandatory sex education programs held the answers to the social crisis created by adolescent sex. With typical liberal myopia, Title X was drafted under the notion that the main reason teenagers got pregnant was because they didn't know enough about sex and reproduction. Supporters of Title X presumed sexual activity among teenagers was acceptable and religious traditions stressing abstinence were antiquated. It presupposed that by emphasizing explicit information on contraceptives and sexually transmitted diseases, the federal government could control human nature in a value-free setting.

Now, more than twenty years and hundreds of millions of federal tax dollars later, the conclusion many researchers have drawn about the effect of Title X is that while some of the programs may have increased knowledge about the subject matter, few help at all with clarification of values and thereby have little impact on sexual behavior amongst teens. To paraphrase an off-color joke, a teenage boy was caught looking at dirty pictures. His father said, "You know, if you keep doing that, you'll go blind." To this the boy replied, "Then I'll just do it 'til I need glasses." Without a context of familial and moral responsibility, the threat of consequences is just one more opportunity to rebel against authority. Some kids will do it simply because you tell them it's a bad idea. Not surprisingly, birth control pills have not protected America's youth from pregnancy. Abortion has increased their emotional scars and suicidal tendencies. Condoms have not protected them from gonorrhea, chlamydia, syphilis, trichomoniasis, or Human Papilloma Virus (HPV).

There are a number of sexually transmitted diseases that may never reveal themselves in the form of symptoms, which means an unsuspecting carrier can go on infecting sexual partners for years to come. HPV (genital warts) is transmitted by simple skin on skin contact, so a condom is no protection, and there is no cure. In the case of chlamydia in women, the disease can quietly destroy their reproductive organs while never manifesting symptoms. Thousands of women who practiced sex freely in their teens and have settled down to start a family in their thirties are discovering they are unable to have children. When the doctor finds the scar tissue and tells them they had an STD, they can only reply in shock, "But I never had any symptoms!"

The Centers for Disease Control and Prevention says that about four million teenagers will contract one or more sexually transmitted diseases this year—despite the fact that clinics funded by Title X screen for STDs and routinely pass out condoms. Dr. Malcolm Potts, one of the inventors of spermicidal lubricated condoms and president of Family Health International concluded, "Telling someone who engages in high-risk behavior to use a condom is like telling someone who is driving drunk to use a seat belt."

VALUE-FREE DIVERSITY

Did you ever see the movie *Clueless*? If you haven't, the plot of the movie is about a popular high school girl who is trying to find herself in the midst of a hectic academic and social life. It is a silly comedy, yet, as with most comedies, it points to some truths about daily life in American public schools.

One of the first things one notices is there are several distinct cliques or groups who roam the campus, each one having its own characteristics—computer geeks, punks, stoners, preppies, jocks, and others.

You can find similar social demarcations on any given campus in the United States.

As with every society, most members of the high school community have an unquenchable desire to belong to something, and each clique has its own unique qualifications for membership that give its members a sense of belonging, an identity that sets the teenager apart from others. Preppies seem to prefer khaki pants and sweaters, while punks like to spike their hair and wear chains or studded belts.

This form of inculcation into society is a healthy thing if the individuals involved are given proper direction. For instance, at my church on Easter morning, my bishop confirmed several people as members of Christ's one Holy and Apostolic Church. Through catechism, counseling, and spiritual direction, these candidates for membership decided they wanted to be part of something larger then they are, with eternal significance—and that is the Church.

In most societies, children are nurtured and trained to act, speak, and dress in certain ways to become successful members of that society, to receive the benefits from working hard, and to feel a sense of worth. While we've heard from various sources that America is a very diverse nation, there are certain truths and ways of living that statistically lead to success. Conversely, there are certain ways of living that statistically lead to poverty, disease, and even death.

Going back to Uncle Sam's high schools and the various groups therein, why are there so many groups, and why does it seem certain factions of those groups are hell-bent on destroying their own lives in one way or the other? Young people believe they are invincible. They think they can take chances and live for the moment without any unfortunate consequences, at least while they are still in school. Let's face it— Mom and Dad are paying the bills, so the cost of their reckless behavior is usually negligible.

If financial and personal success are the prime motivations for attending high school, why is it so many young people seem to make purposeful choices that are so self-destructive? Why is it that these same teenagers choose to join groups that are averse to making the decisions that lead to success?

In *Why Johnny Can't Tell Right from Wrong*, author William Kirkpatrick explores this problem and points to the curriculum of the American public school system. He states that there are two different philosophies in education competing with each other, one being "character building" and the other being the much more progressive "decision making." Unfortunately for our school children, the latter of the two has been winning the culture war for the last three decades.

The "character building" view focuses on teaching virtue, a word not heard much on any campus today. A virtue is a moral quality external to the person, and the individual practicing this virtue shapes his character to it. Interestingly enough, it comes from the Latin root *virtut*, which refers to strength or manliness. This is ironic, given that much of the leadership in public schools seems determined to emasculate its young men and turn them into wimps who will not stand up for anything.

A list of virtues from days gone by would have included chastity, fidelity, honesty, courage, courtesy, and loyalty. These are all admirable traits, traits we would all love to have ingrained in the hearts and minds of our children, but when was the last time you heard a public school standing up for chastity? It is certainly not viewed as an ideal, even when it might serve a simply utilitarian purpose such as stopping the spread of sexually transmitted diseases. Many abstinence programs have had to fight school boards and administrations to get their message across to teenagers because many liberal educators claim abstinence is a virtue dispersed from religious belief. Yet, abstinence is the only sure way of avoiding AIDS, herpes, and other STDs. Put differently, the only 100 percent successful method of birth control is to take the Pill—and hold it between your knees.

Fidelity is not spoken of either as it might offend those who come from broken homes. While it is unfortunate that the divorce rate is high, we must not abandon the ideal of marriage and fidelity as we educate our children. Parents must always expose children to the highest virtues. Children must emulate the hero, not the narcissist, to escape negative circumstances.

The more liberal educational philosophy of "decision making" prefers the word "value" when referring to anything that might have the sound of morality. Values and virtues are different—the latter, as we've just noted, involves objective standards. Values on the other hand are subjective, coming from the individual, not an external source. This is why when public schools must speak of morality at all, they choose the language of "values"—at least then it's not binding. A subjective "value" poses no real threat; it stands for nothing. Because its meaning depends on the individual, it can be anything to anyone at any given time—while still sounding good and moral to the general public. According to Webster's dictionary, value can mean many things, but each meaning given focuses around the word "relative." "Relative worth, utility, or importance: degree of excellence." Be it money or morals, the value of anything is based upon one's own perception. Just like money, morality in this context is based on the market value, or what worth society will assign to it.

I recently pulled up my daughter's former school district's website to see what values they offered in their various public schools. First of all, it was very difficult to determine exactly what they taught for there was very little up front about curriculum. A course description on "tolerance" was the only one highlighted; apparently, this was one of their values. I then decided to look at some of the websites of individual schools in the district. One school focused on four values: unity, pride, respect, and citizenship. Frankly, I've never heard of these as virtues, although they can be good qualities to possess if presented in the right context. The real problem is that these aren't really virtues of any sort;

rather, they are feel-good words that blur the lines of right and wrong in favor of the good of the many. For example, it is a great thing to have unity in society, but it requires that its citizens share and agree on certain basic beliefs about life. What beliefs are these particular schools espousing that warrant the students to be unified? Are they to be unified in the belief that God and his laws are immutable? Probably not. Perhaps they are to be unified in the belief that there are no absolutes? More likely.

I don't need to say much about "pride" except to say "pride goeth before a fall." No doubt, we should take pride in our work, but in what else should we take pride? Parents and Friends of Lesbians and Gays would say that students should have pride about their sexuality, gay pride in particular. By the way, when was the last time you heard any students forming clubs around the notion of heterosexual pride? If the liberals gain power in our country, that day might not be too far off.

The values of "respect" and "citizenship" should receive the same scrutinizing from parents. Respect for what? Life and the unborn child? Respect for alternative lifestyles? Respect for women who murder their husbands for being abusive? And what does citizenship involve? For many teachers, that would mean making sure students do not recite "under God" in the Pledge of Allegiance. Further, "citizen" and "citizenship" don't necessarily function well together. During the Cold War, forty million Soviet citizens were murdered because they didn't practice good citizenship.

Furthermore, on the marquee of the web page entitled "Information" for one school, I was surprised to find what appeared to be the district's most important messages to parents and students. No, it wasn't "In God We Trust" or "Life, Liberty, and the Pursuit of Happiness." Instead, it stated, "[This] Is a Tobacco Free School District." Oh, thank God . . . oops, I meant to say, thank the *surgeon general* for such a profound remark. Now, I'm certain that our children will be preserved because they know tobacco is as evil as owning a gun.

Going back to Kirkpatrick's argument that there are two philosophies of education, the "character building" view is based on virtues, which are drawn from a system of morality that is fixed and unchangeable. This system does not receive its value from society; rather, it is external to society and comes from a final arbitrator whose name is God.

Uncle Sam's view of "decision making" believes the opposite: individuals determine morality and values are relative to every new situation in which that individual finds himself. Certainly there is no outside imposition of virtue on the person; that would be oppressive and imperialistic. No, the student being trained under this notion is persuaded to believe he is his own god—and how dare anyone tell him what to do!

In the end, children in this kind of teaching environment are left to make up their own minds; unfortunately, most of them are left in a quandary and will ultimately end up making the choice most beneficial to them, no matter how immoral. In fact, Kirkpatrick points to the fact that many of the sex and drug education courses based on the "decision making" model only encourage students to participate in drug use and illicit sex.

Without virtues and a character building view of education, schools can expect their students to continue to join cliques that encourage their members to make decisions that are detrimental to their future success. Without heroes and role models who demonstrate those virtues, and without those virtues being promoted in public schools so that children are actually encouraged to find and emulate those heroes, these students will continue to follow a path that leads to poverty, disease, and destruction.

Identity is crucial to teenagers; to deny it or to tell kids they don't need to worry about it is being, at best, naive. Children are not born with the inclinations to be skinheads or stoners, drug dealers or gangbangers. They have been conditioned by their surroundings. A lack of proper direction, guidance, and moral authority not only provides a disservice to our school children but also leads them to disaster.

TALKING LOUD, LEARNING NOTHING

They sit on the wall. They stare out in space. They eat lunch together, smoke cigarettes together, cry about racism together. But study together? No way. That's "acting white." Somewhere between the civil rights movement and the expansion of Uncle Sam's "Great Society," the quest for African-Americans to aspire to academic excellence was lost. With hundreds of historically black colleges and universities, founded immediately after emancipation, graduating thousands of successful doctors and lawyers, prestigious scholars, prominent scientists, authors, teachers, and businessmen, the growing rejection of structured education by today's inner city black youth highlights a new and alarming black phenomenon.

This is clearly not a question of whether African-Americans can learn scientific or mathematical concepts. Black educational patterns for the first one hundred years after slavery are evidence they can. Nor is it a question of whether they can escape poverty if they finish high school. The Bureau of Labor Statistics notes that, in 1980, 92 percent of black women with a high school education and 86 percent of black males with a high school diploma had family incomes greater than twice the poverty line. Economically the black middle class experienced unprecedented success during the 1980s. The number of black professionals increased 63 percent between 1980 and 1988 while black managers and officers in corporate America increased by 30 percent. Clearly, the question has nothing to do with potential and everything to do with the values being promoted in education today.

The idea that government was mandated to find remedies to wipe out racism evolved into political correctness to placate blacks. It wasn't enough that the "black power" movement symbolized black beauty. No, everything mainstream—including education—had to be reviled as "establishment," which in the poor communities meant it was anti-black. Racism was suspected in all learning materials, and standardized tests were thereby determined to be inappropriate to administer to blacks. Elite blacks in academia focused most of their energies on uprooting Western culture from all curricula. The books *Native Son* by Richard Wright and *The Fire Next Time* by James Baldwin became mandatory reading. *I Know Why the Caged Bird Sings* by Maya Angelou and *To Kill a Mockingbird* by Harper Lee are still revered in public high schools today.

The message to whites was that acknowledgement of black suffrage must be incorporated into every subject in order to atone for slavery. The message to blacks who accepted the status quo, excelled in their studies, and mastered the "King's English" was that they had sold out their race. Those who respected their white teachers were categorized as having a slave mentality. I remember hearing and heeding this message when I was in middle school. Upon arriving from Japan in East St. Louis, Illinois, in 1969, after being far removed from the racial dynamics of the marches and death of Dr. King, I wanted, like most adolescents, to fit in. To hear black leaders declare that the essence of Afrocentrism was rebellion against the establishment was my ticket to acceptance, and I had a great excuse to dissent.

East St. Louis embodied what was wrong with America. As mentioned in Chapter Two, we lived just across the Mississippi River from where the infamous *Dred Scott* decision was argued, and black and white relationships were tense. Whites had abandoned the public schools for private schools in the area because the government was insisting on mandatory integration and was passing busing regulations. By the time we relocated, the "white plight" had created conditions in my school where all the students were black and all the teachers were white. My neighborhood was typical of most cities and towns where blacks were isolated from commerce and decent housing. Destitute, dirty, used, and stripped of the resources that had once flourished in the area, we were no longer progressing toward middle class.

The military in which my dad served for twenty years had brought us there following his tour in Vietnam only to notify us that housing at Scott Air Force Base was "first-come-first-served," and a whole lot of white families were coming up first. It was there that I first learned how to make a Molotov cocktail, how to smoke weed, and how to challenge a cop to make me a martyr for black pride. It was there that I also learned that the only blacks in education worthy of their souls were those who went inside to turn the establishment upside down.

Rather than moving toward a more cohesive learning environment, the obsessive emphasis on race was pulling blacks away from education altogether. Starting with isolationist black history, black student centers, and black clubs just forty years after the landmark *Brown v. Board of Education* decision, when Chief Justice Warren concluded that segregation on the basis of race deprived blacks of equal education, blacks rejected not only the integrated institutions but also the very education of the institutions.

Attempts to uproot racism from public education have come a long way since the 1970s. Racial rhetoric has been refined far beyond multiculturalism courses and where one stands on affirmative action. Today, acceptable speech about race matters must toe the line of liberalism in every area, or else it is anathema. Children educated in public schools are taught more about classification into specific minority groups than about virtue and honor. Minority groups today of course mean blacks, women, homosexuals, Hispanics, and a few blanks reserved for future groups liberals decide to deem as victims. Rest assured it will never include white males or Christians. The focus of public education is not to teach values but political correctness, to prepare children to accept a mindset that includes set-aside programs for certain minorities.

Note that "minority" has little to do with actual numbers. Ethnic groups with fewer members than some of the aforementioned groups are totally excluded from consideration for special preferences even though they align themselves politically with the Left. Neither Asians nor Jews qualify for minority status with regards to affirmative action disbursements. Public education is not just about reading, writing, and arithmetic or learning to adjust as a minority. Now it's about a political agenda to predetermine a code of ethics wherein one sees poverty as predicated on position or social status. If a code of ethics promotes self-initiative or what the Left calls a "boot strap mentality," it is considered racist.

In his best-selling book, *Losing the Race*, linguist and Berkeley Professor John McWhorter makes two suggestions to get blacks back on track academically. During his controversial observations at the height of debates on affirmative action and ebonics, McWhorter pointed out that "the first phase of the Civil Rights Movement was to level the proverbial playing field" and that this job is nearly accomplished. After years of challenging what he calls "the cult of victimology" with hundreds of his black students and in his book, McWhorter notes that it is not enough for blacks to be treated as equals "but that the second phase for blacks to progress is to get out there and play, and in order for that to be worthwhile, or even possible . . . we must allow ourselves to be treated as equals."

McWhorter first suggests that blacks no longer look at their successes as anecdotes but as the norm.

> Too often the black family with a beautiful house, nice cars, and children in private school is processed as an exception and almost an inconvenience, the idea seeming to be that to pay too much attention to this "B. Smith" kind of person will distract from the grinding horror of life for 99 percent of the race . . . yet only one in five black people [actually] live in the inner city, and only one in four black families

[actually] live below the poverty line. That's not perfect, but progress is being made and fast.

The second suggestion is for blacks to recognize that an occasional inconvenience is not oppression and to constantly claim such impedes progress towards equality. "The person who one considers incapable of coping with any hardship whatsoever, who one considers capable of achievement only under ideal conditions, is someone one pities, cares for, and perhaps even likes, but is not someone one respects, and thus is someone one does not truly consider an equal." McWhorther addresses these challenges that blacks must reconcile individually to succeed amidst any circumstances or trials. Still both of his suggestions make certain values assumptions, and, given the current state of family breakdown, it may be too late.

DUMBED DOWN

Family breakdown in black America has opened the door to meaningless concepts of class and cultural warfare that have distracted inner city youths from personal responsibility. The failure of family formation to pass on the values that helped blacks survive for decades has taken a horrible toll in most urban neighborhoods. Random murder stalks the streets. My secretary's sixteen-year-old brother experienced such a fate. The stray bullets of gang clashes claim the lives of infants and passersby. My bank manager's son was gunned down at twenty-three during a routine errand to the grocery store.

The essence of life has been reduced to meaninglessness, and our public school system promotes the idea. Much of the government establishment has adopted the notion that public education's purpose is to disseminate techniques and formulas in a value-free environment. Children are viewed as biological matter that can be taught how to process value-neutral information and material to help them develop a career and earn money later in life. On this front, public education has assisted the popular culture in transmitting the message that the point of life is acquisition. Uncle Sam targeted low-income families to develop new plans for cradle-to-grave care that start in public education. Programs such as Head Start and Healthy Start are no longer designed to impart reading through phonics or nutrition through proper diet but to promote indoctrination of a political philosophy to modify behavior.

On the horns of liberal policy, government attempted to redefine its role to cover all areas of life, including health, work, leisure, and death. Parents and families were no longer assumed primary caregivers or competent enough to raise children without government oversight, and government was getting their fingers into everything from nutritional requirements to those "do not remove" labels on mattresses. Education bureaucrats have been empowered with the responsibility to remind parents about everything from vaccinations to bedtimes. Welfare families are subjected to surveys to protect the children from potential developmental delays. Legislative bills were introduced in California pushing for family screening at the time each child is born. One of the bills stated that years of experience had taught "the most effective strategies to combat child abuse are those that begin very early in a child's life, preferably when a child is a newborn."

The problem is that the assumptions used by most government agencies—agencies created to protect children—imply that the traditional family is the enemy. The image of the out-of-control social worker falsely accusing innocent parents and yanking children out of the arms of screaming mothers is nearly as ingrained in the public psyche as the disgruntled postal worker. Rarely do these agencies acknowledge that unmarried households and the lack of principled, value-friendly curricula in school might be part of the problem.

Under the Elementary and Secondary Education Act schools are being encouraged to set up one-stop shopping centers to provide federally funded services of preschool, health clinics, social services, parent education, welfare assistance, family counseling, and outcome assessments. Educational concepts such as Goals 2000 were intro-duced to help Uncle Sam's children select career paths. Many people view the one-stop shopping for government services as a progressive move to promote efficiency, but education should not be about lower-ing standards to make life easier for the poor. Proper education is the confirmation of a virtue system consistent with personal responsi-bility, proper family formation, and civil society.

NO CHILD LEFT BEHIND

In a major effort to overcome the huge inequalities between school dis-tricts across the nation, President George Bush signed into law the No Child Left Behind Act of 2001 (NCLB). A reauthorization of the original Elementary and Secondary Education Act signed in 1965 as part of President Lyndon B. Johnson's New Society program, NCLB was designed to provide increased accountability in public schools based on a results-oriented system of federal management and funding.

President Bush was responding to the public concern over educa-tion and a rash of poor test results by American students. His focus was on those students who were "falling through the cracks," who, prima-rily, were in the inner-city districts of the larger metropolitan areas such as Los Angeles, Atlanta, and Washington D.C. As previously discussed, students in these districts are the most at-risk, living in a culture of aban-donment, drugs, and violence. All too often these children find them-selves not in a position of fighting through hours of homework and managing their time between piano lessons and baseball, but rather, fighting to stay alive as they walk home from school. Many are so inun-dated with a culture of death and depravity that they have absolutely no sense of themselves or of any destiny outside the ghetto in which they live. These students are most susceptible to being left behind academically and professionally.

No Child Left Behind was designed with these students in mind. Still, you can lead a horse to water, but you can't make him study. Any federal solution that doesn't address root social causes will have limited success. In this case, "federal solution" is probably an oxymoron, since the only possible solution will be found in a return to strong families and the social activism of religious absolutes energized by scriptural commands to help others. While NCLB may appear on paper to hold failing public schools accountable, both academically and fiscally, it perpetuates the same crippling mentality of the government (federal and state) being the nanny or father-figure for the children of the nation. Furthermore, federal educational programs such as NCLB tend to overlook the real issues facing students in inner city districts, namely those topics regarding morality, family, and society.

In its most robust form, in addition to academic learning, education is the transmission of a community's values and virtues from one generation to the next, with the express purpose of ensuring that the family and community will stay intact and survive for future generations. By providing boundaries and a sense of security and protection to each succeeding generation, adults create an environment where children can imagine a better future for themselves.

It is no accident or blind act of discrimination that the Hebrews held certain biblical laws on sexuality for thousands of years. Not only were they ordained by God, they were and are laws that prevent sexually transmitted diseases, untimely pregnancies, and even death. Unfortunately, in today's inner city school systems, there is no cohesive set of values by which children are instructed to govern their lives. Clint Bolick writes in his book, *Transformations: The Promise and Politics of Empowerment*, "[P]ublic schools have undermined the common school ideal, not only in their racial and economic isolation but in their violent environments and in their failure to transmit shared American values."

In fact, in many of these schools, children are taught that any form of morality is acceptable as long as one is safe. That's similar to saying, "It's okay to cheat, Johnny, just don't get caught!" Many school children are introduced to birth control at a very young age in inner city public schools, and abortion is not even considered a threat to the lives of young women. So-called experts on teenage sexuality, who claim it is impossible to expect children to keep their pants on, deride abstinence programs.

Technical solutions, not spiritual or moral answers, are the only ones being offered by the government and its respective public schools in the inner city. Instead of encouraging children to respect their bodies as sacred, our state-run educational system offers condoms, safe sex, and alternative lifestyles. Instead of seeing abstinence as tenable and reasonable, public school officials either encourage sexual experimentation or have their hands tied by liberal groups who demand that anything *besides* a cohesive set of traditional mores is appropriate to teach to our children. Bereft of moral and spiritual guidance, many children are left to find their own way, with no one except perhaps a struggling single mother to help them.

In the best-case scenario of an inner city public school student, his or her parents are still alive and married, one or both is employed, and neither does drugs. Now this is truly a rarity in, say, Compton, California. Even in the best of circumstances, these students still have to contend with the school and neighborhood climate in which they find themselves every day. While the student's parents may espouse honesty, fidelity, and a strong work ethic, the student is still faced with a despairing local scene offering little more than poverty and death. Further-more, the student must then attend a public school for seven to eight hours a day where teachers are more likely than not espousing a political and societal view contrary to that of his or her parents. For the parent who is trying to raise a child in the inner city, she must compete with the public school, which has, either by default or design, taken over the job of parenting. Let's face it: the few hours we spend at home with our children at night and on the weekends is nothing compared to the amount of time given to schools to influence our children's views on sexuality, religion, and morality in general. For a large percentage of children in the inner city, concern for academic success comes last on their list of priorities, by little or no fault of their own.

No Child Left Behind and other government-enacted programs designed to save the failing public educational system naively assume that academics are the most crucial aspect of education and if we can hold schools and districts accountable through federal mandates, children in the inner city will miraculously leave the cycle of poverty. We've once again assumed that a technical solution will be the cure-all for a disease requiring a moral and spiritual remedy. It is the failure of the public school system to transmit common, traditional moral values to its students and bolster rather than contradict the values of their parents that helps to ensure that the prison of destitution remains a permanent institution in the inner city.

No Child Left Behind has no power to coerce public schools into providing a particular moral education, nor should it. This has always been the responsibility of the family and the religious community, and to impede their mission has been the sad and tragic legacy of inner city public schools. Giving the government more power to regulate the educational system only feeds the cycle of poverty, perpetuating a technical solution that cannot solve anything. Until we are willing to demand that our federal and state officials give up their control over the lives of our children and take responsibility for that control ourselves, children will continue to slip through the cracks socially and spiritually. And when the government comes along with stiffer regulations to "remedy" the problem, further eroding our freedoms, we will have no one to blame but ourselves.

7

OPM (Other People's Money)

America in its earliest days attracted people from all over the world for one simple reason: freedom. Freedom wasn't just about the right to say what you want or casting a ballot in an election; freedom meant having the liberty to make something of your life. It was a freedom unlike any other, not to be found in Europe—or anywhere else for that matter. In Europe, if you were born rich, you tended to die rich, and more important, if you were born poor, you usually died poor. Children of royalty most often stayed royalty, and children of field hands most often stayed in the field. But not in America. There was no royalty, and nobody had to work for anybody else for very long unless that was what they wanted, except for the slaves, who were forced laborers for the first eighty-seven years of America's official founding.

In America, there was upward mobility of the kind never seen before in the history of the world, and it was largely facilitated by land. Lots of land. All a sharecropper in America had to do was go west to find new land to farm, and pretty soon, he was a landowner. The fact that anyone with enough drive could succeed allowed people—even those who came over as indentured servants—to be free from dependency on anyone, government or otherwise.

None of this tremendous expansion would have been possible if the government had meddled in the economy or taxed Americans into serfdom. American government officials did not get rich on the backs of taxpayers; they did it by leaving government after a few years of service and making money in the free market.

To the extent government intervened at all, it was largely to protect slaveholders. Laws had to be rigged and police had to be used to enforce the slavery system—all under official sanction and protection of government. Frederic Bastiat, the godfather of social thought regarding individual freedom and renowned author of *The Law*, wrote in 1850,

> There are only two issues, slavery and tariffs, where, contrary to the general spirit of the republic of the United States, law has assumed the character of a plunderer. Slavery is a violation, by law, of liberty. The protective tariff is a violation, by law, of property. It is a most remarkable fact that this double legal crime—a sorrowful inheritance from the Old World—should be the only issue that can, and perhaps will, lead to the ruin of the Union. It is indeed impossible to imagine, at the very heart of a society, a more astounding fact than this: the law has come to be an instrument of injustice.

Had it not been for the heavy hand of government, slavery could not have remained the blight that it was in America for as long as it did. But the heavy hand had a long reach. President Lincoln may have issued the Emancipation Proclamation back in 1863, but in the twentieth century, slavery—albeit of a different stripe—made a real comeback.

Uncle Sam started building his own plantation with OPM, other people's money, stealing the resources of the rich in order to enslave the poor. The brilliance of it—if you want to call it that—is that the real result is hidden from view. Who would initially suspect taxing the rich actually hurts the poor? It seems only logical that if large numbers of the wealthy support the system, not only are they best able to afford the onerous taxes but also they get to placate their guilty consciences in the process.

This new plantation system expanded mostly in two periods during which the government grew more than all others combined: the New Deal and the Great Society. Although the history books praise both as important successes that saved the poor and the working class, these programs actually wreaked havoc on both the economy and the poor. Desperate times call for desperate measures, but unless you get exhaustive analysis of potential impacts and have an exit strategy from those measures, your solution can end up causing as much or more harm than the original problem, especially when the government controls the reins. Like a castaway who uses all the wood on an island to build fires and then has none left to build a boat, politicians are notoriously short-sighted.

President Franklin D. Roosevelt began implementing his ambitious New Deal programs shortly after taking office in 1933. Millions of Americans went on the federal dole in short order, but despite FDR's reforms, the Great Depression kept getting worse. The bottom of the slump was not actually felt until 1938; the economy just got worse and worse, only picking up with the prospect of World War II.

Following in FDR's misguided footsteps, President Lyndon B. Johnson created the Great Society, which was anything but great for the poor. Dramatic expansion of welfare was the centerpiece, but there were many other components. Cash grants, food stamps, Medicaid, housing subsidies, and all the other assorted goodies granted by the government temporarily aided the poor but made them increasingly dependent on Uncle Sam. And Uncle Sam kept the poor at his mercy by feeding them the opiate of free money but also robbing them of economic opportunities indirectly by taxing and regulating the rich, whose capital must be circulated to maintain a strong economy.

Now, seventy years after the Great Depression, Uncle Sam and his fifty-one nephews, counting the District of Columbia as part of the family, have continued raising taxes and increasing the burdens of red tape on businesses. As the collective government plantation has expanded, there is less room for people to find land to call their own and build upon.

The main thrust of the New Deal and the Great Society, and liberal policy between and since those periods, was to help the poor by taxing the rich, but the most prominent of those taxes (the capital gains tax, the corporate income tax, and the death tax) hurt the poor. Even laws intended to help the poor directly, such as rent control, licensing regulations to protect consumers, and minimum wage or "living wage" laws, have hurt those they were intended to help. Regulation does this by driving up costs for businesses and prices for consumers. It also makes the hurdles for entrepreneurship so high it becomes nearly impossible for the people with fewer resources to clear them. Wage laws actually hurt the lower-income workers by forcing businesses to cut costs by hiring fewer employees or by creating metropolitan delocalization, which pushes second-income housewives and well-off suburban teenagers into the competition pool for those small number of jobs.

CAPITALISM 101

In a free market system, the most tried-and-true method for the poor to become rich is through entrepreneurship on the playing field of capitalism. When markets are open, people with little more than determination and a sharp mind can become as successful as those handed every opportunity in life and with a silver spoon wedged firmly in their mouths. Entrepreneurs create ideas for investors to launch while capitalism opens the doors for the money to flow freely. Contrary to what the media elites would have you believe, this is not just true for white kids. The American dream is open to all Americans.

Look at the success of the late Reginald Francis Lewis, chairman, CEO, and principal shareholder of TLC Beatrice International Holdings Inc., until his untimely death at fifty-one of brain cancer in January 1993. Born on December 7, 1942, in East Baltimore at a time when black people couldn't shop or even try on clothes at many downtown stores, eat in certain restaurants, or go to certain movie theaters, young Lewis lived the title of his autobiography, *Why Should White Guys Have All the Fun*. A successful corporate lawyer who remade himself into a financier and buyer of corporations, Lewis bought McCall Pattern Company for $22.5 million, guided it to record earnings, sold it for $65 million, and then went on to leverage a buyout of Beatrice International Foods, a global giant with sixty-four companies in thirty-one countries, for just under a billion dollars. Despite all his hard efforts, he wouldn't have achieved all he did had it not been for capital investors.

Look at Robert Johnson, the founder of Black Entertainment Television. He rose from humble means to become a billionaire. He toiled for decades, building a media empire from scratch. He had a vision of a cable channel specifically targeted to blacks—a vision no one else had at the time. Despite all his efforts, he wouldn't have succeeded without investors. He took an initial investment of $15,000 and turned it into a $3 billion operation when he sold BET to Viacom in 2000.

Investment, particularly venture capital given to small start-ups, is the ultimate transfer of wealth from rich to poor. Investors care little about the size of entrepreneurs' bank accounts or the color of their skin. They make their decision about whether or not to pour money into a company based on the vision, talent, and dedication of the people running it. When government punishes people for the act of investing, fewer entrepreneurs are going to get a chance to get the funding they need to make their dreams a reality. For all the crying black politicians do over economic stimulus in urban America, entrepreneurs are still the number one creators of new businesses and new jobs, thereby under-

scoring the need for limited taxation and regulation over business owners and private investors.

As any dictionary defines it, capitalism is an economic system in
which private individuals or groups of individuals own land, factories,
and other means of production. They compete with one another using
the hired labor of other people to produce goods and services for
profit. Liberals always whine about "big business" (read "large corporations"), even when Democrats are feeding at the corporate trough,
and seem determined to punish them for being successful. They hate
the fact that in the world of capitalism there will be winners and losers, but such is the nature of competition and business, acquisition and
ambition. Investors play a role, as do entrepreneurs, and when businesses do well, most everyone does well. Thus, when government is
excessive in its regulation or taxation of investors or entrepreneurs, the
whole of society suffers, particularly underprivileged communities
which are hit hardest when the money stops flowing downward.
Capitalism isn't about the concentration of wealth with its power and
influence in the hands of a few. In an open and competitive market
environment, anyone can participate. And anyone who works hard and
never gives up can win.

Punishing the strong players in a capitalist system punishes everyone, including consumers. And those consumers hurt the most are
those who spend the highest proportion of their incomes on food, shelter, and other necessities—namely the poor. Most established corporations get all their money from consumers. Even the money they get
from other corporations comes from consumers because that's how the
other corporations got their money. When corporations (and don't
think "big business" because that's only a fraction of all corporations)
pay income taxes, they get the money that generates Uncle Sam's tax
revenue from one source: consumers.

Taxing and regulating corporations doesn't just hurt the poor by
raising prices; it is outrageous in principle. Every dollar a corporation

makes over expenses gets taxed. When employees get their salaries, they pay taxes. When the executives get bonuses, they pay taxes. When profits are shared with shareholders as dividends, they pay taxes. The corporate income tax really amounts to double taxation. That money they're paying Uncle Sam is money they're not reinvesting in their company or using to hire new employees. That means slower growth, fewer jobs, and a weaker economy—all because of taxes.

Now if you're thinking you don't want to help corporate America, you should think about what you mean by "corporate America." Corporate America is not just giants like General Motors; it's also owners of convenience stores and hair salons—and every company in-between. Besides, what is so wrong with helping General Motors anyway? If you tax General Motors, that drives up the prices of the cars they sell, which hurts most the people least able to afford a new car. Even if GM doesn't pay high income taxes, it's because they hired an army of accountants to maximize tax shelters, which drives up their costs and prices. Excessively taxing and regulating GM to punish its success means, for example, a thirty-year-old factory worker, Bernie, will have to settle for a less safe and less efficient used car because Uncle Sam drove up the price on the car he wants by $1,000, making it too expensive for him to afford.

EXCESSIVE TAXATION

Bastiat summarized slavery, tariffs, protections, welfare, subsidies, public guarantees, and excessive taxation in two words: legal plunder. He describes legal plunder as "organized injustice." A closer examination of Bastiat is necessary to put America's tax code into a specific framework as it relates to capitalism, investments, and business today. Taxes in proper context are simply redistribution of OPM, and Bastiat explains with simplicity how to identify this legal plunder. Keep in mind that he penned these words in 1850:

> See if the law takes from some persons what belongs to them, and gives it to other persons to whom it does not belong. See if the law benefits one citizen at the expense of another by doing what the citizen himself cannot do without committing a crime.
>
> You say: "There are persons who have no money," and you turn to the law. But the law is not a breast that fills itself with milk. Nor are the lacteal veins of the law supplied with milk from a source outside the society. Nothing can enter the public treasury for the benefit of one citizen or one class unless other citizens and other classes have been forced to send it in. If every person draws from the treasury the amount that he has put in it, it is true that the law then plunders nobody. But this procedure does nothing for the persons who have no money. It does not promote equality of income. The law can be an instrument of equalization only as it takes from some persons and gives to other persons. When the law does this, it is an instrument of plunder.
>
> You say: "There are persons who lack education" and you turn to the law. But the law is not, in itself, a torch of learning that shines its light abroad. The law extends over a society where some persons have knowledge and others do not; where some citizens need to learn, and others can teach. In this matter of education, the law has only two alternatives: it can permit this transaction of teaching-and-learning to operate freely and without the use of force, or it can force human wills in this matter by taking from some of them enough to pay the teachers who are appointed by government to instruct others, without charge. But in this second case, the law commits legal plunder by violating liberty and property.
>
> You say: "Here are persons who are lacking in morality or religion," and you turn to the law. But law is force. And need I point out

what a violent and futile effort it is to use force in the matters of morality and religion?

What Bastiat is saying is that no one is simply entitled to acquisitions. They come through ambition and work. Acquisitions and acquirements do not equal entitlement, whether welfare or education,
healthcare or Social Security. And for a government to purchase acquisitions or acquirements for someone by taking other people's money
under threat of force is wrong. It's theft; the fact that the thief has an
IRS business card instead of a ski mask makes little difference.

Although taxes have become a part of modern existence that is as
inevitable as death, it is time for us to question their morality, and in
some cases even their legality. Most of all we should question their
inevitability. I look forward to a day in the not-too-distant future under
the banner of a smaller, more efficient government when we will be
able to say, "There's only one thing certain in this world: death."

Capital Gains Tax

Capital gains taxes are the harshest fiscal punishment a liberal
government can inflict, and they have the net effect of limiting the
number of rags-to-riches success stories. Investors already face a dicey
proposition whenever they invest in a start-up venture; just look at
the financial carnage from the dot-bomb nightmare. Taking a large
chunk of whatever profits they do earn makes an investor much less
likely to invest, particularly in a risky venture. People who run risky
ventures often don't have much money, however, and some of the
highest risk opportunities are the ones that would improve inner-city
neighborhoods.

When investors pay taxes on capital gains, they have less money
to invest in new enterprises, and between huge losses in some investments and punitive taxes on the successful ones, there's less room for
error for investors. Where's the first place they're going to retract their

investments? From business ventures in high-risk inner-city neighborhoods and those headed by first-time entrepreneurs.

The process is simple: taxes go up, investment goes down, jobs are lost, wealthy people stop taking risks, and the economy stagnates. Please let us get over these foolish notions that capital gains taxes only impact the wealthy. Not only do over 33 percent of Americans with incomes below $30,000 own stock, and hence pay capital gains taxes, but these taxes hurt every person who is financially downstream from that wealthy person because he or she is less willing to take risks. This slows the flow of money downward creating the economic stagnation mentioned above. The wealthiest members of our society should be encouraged to take risks by eliminating the capital gains tax. Our country was built on and thrives on risk. The alternative is to keep their taxes high, thereby ensuring the rich will hold onto their money instead of risking it on investment. By eliminating capital gains taxes, politicians could help energize a flagging economy, bring additional revenues into Washington, and help both middle-class investors and workers.

Expect the liberal politicians to complain when there's less extra money floating around for them to spend; bellyaching about deficits is a given. Two things are important to recall when the whining commences: First, it's not the politicians' money to begin with; it's the taxpayers', the people who *earned* it. Politicians have no right to complain if tax cuts decrease their petty cash. Second, the revenue falloff is only temporary. As the history of Ronald Reagan's and John F. Kennedy's tax rate reductions proves, federal revenues actually grow when federal rates are substantially reduced. This is because economies are dynamic. And when new money becomes available for investment and job creation, the economy, instead of being gobbled whole by federal overhead and misdirection, actually grows, creating more and higher incomes. The real culprit behind deficits is uncontrolled federal spending and the presumption of politicians that it is their money to spend however they please.

That said, it is also important to remember that tax cuts are not magical. This is a national economy, after all, not Harry Potter's Hogwarts. The GOP found this out the hard way after overselling the Bush tax cut in 2001. According to Eric Schlecht, Director of Congressional Relations for the 335,000-member National Taxpayers Union (NTU), "Republican supporters did make a major strategic blunder when they argued that the 2001 Bush tax cut would have an *immediate* stimulative effect on the economy" (emphasis added). NTU's research showed that since most of the marginal rate reductions will happen in 2004 and later, the effect of the early years of the tax cut is far too small to have any substantial effect on economic incentives. Schlecht said that "to think otherwise is either pure folly or wanton self-delusion."

The idea that the $300 and $600 rebates of 2001 might boost the economy turned out to be equally delusional. Schlecht continues,

> The failure of President Ford's rebates to stimulate the economy in the mid-70s, and Nobel Laureate economist Milton Friedman's research proving that such quick fixes don't work, should have convinced Congress of that.
>
> The current economic slowdown was a result of decreased investment, not consumption. In fact, until very recently consumer confidence remained high and consumption levels were steady. The problem lies in the business sector's unwillingness to continue investment on a sufficient level after the recent market correction. The economy needs a boost in investment, savings, and stock values.

And how do we get this boost? This is where a capital gains tax cut comes into play. Schlect says such a cut "would provide just that by lowering the costs associated with the creation of capital and investment, and by increasing economic incentives."

While many liberal thinkers on Capitol Hill and in the press repeatedly said cutting the capital gains tax would seriously reduce revenues, an increasing body of evidence would seem to suggest otherwise. Since these analysts are unwilling to include economic incentives created by cutting capital gains taxes in their calculations, and the possible impact of those incentives on the economy, they consistently overestimate the projected revenue cost of cutting capital gains taxes. In fact, according to calculations by IRS and the U.S. Senate's Joint Economic Committee staff, the evidence demonstrates that a capital gains tax cut causes little or no reduction in revenues, especially when tracked across multiple years.

Schlect goes on to cite a study by Standard and Poor's that stated that the 1997 capital gains tax cut, which was signed by Bill Clinton, gave a significant boost to economic growth and stock prices. They also found that additional revenues from raised stock prices, increased turnover, and faster growth totally offset the revenue losses projected from the reduced capital gains tax rate. "Of greater importance to President Bush," he notes, "are the findings of the Club for Growth's Steve Moore. An economist and long time Washington observer, Moore found that capital gains tax cuts actually increase revenues in the short term. His research found that the lower capital gains rate after the 1997 tax cut yielded 80 percent more revenue over the following four-year period than was projected if the rate had remained at its 1997 level."

This discussion is also relevant to another tax recently in the headlines—the double taxation of dividend income. According to IRS statistics, 46 percent of taxpayers claiming dividends on their 2000 returns had less than $50,000 in adjusted gross income, while 64 percent had less than $50,000 in wage and salary income only.

As in the case of capital gains, the rising ownership of stock among working-class and middle-class households is also augmented by common-sense economics: more capital to invest in the private sector leads to more business creation and eventually more job creation. Cutting taxes on capital gains can serve as the catalyst to restart this cycle.

A capital gains tax cut is neither a tax cut for the rich nor for big business. It will not lead to inflation or an overheated economy. Instead it will help provide the economic stimulus our country so badly needs. Uncle Sam should move to immediately and significantly reduce the capital gains tax, or better yet, eliminate it altogether.

Corporate Income and Payroll Taxes

By the National Taxpayers Union's reckoning, in 2002, federal, state, and local governments collected over $178 billion in corporate income taxes, or the equivalent of $618 for each person living in the U.S. Many individuals believe that figure represents $178 billion that the rest of us don't have to pay. Some critics believe corporations should pay even more in taxes. On the surface, taxing corporations instead of people may sound appealing. However, it's not that simple, since corporations are people working as a legal entity. The corporate response to higher taxes is not benign—it takes the form of higher prices, lower payments to stockholders, or reduced employee compensation and capital investment. You can't hurt a company without hurting the people who work for it and buy from it.

Under any of these options, hard-working Americans end up paying the tax either through lower wages if they work for a corporation, poorer performance if they own shares in a mutual fund, or higher prices when they purchase a product. This tax burden doesn't show up on any pay slip or price tag, however, so it is more difficult to quantify and track.

Corporate taxes impose an even greater burden because they represent double taxation. When a company earns a profit, it pays taxes on that money. When it pays its stockholders a dividend, that same money is taxed again. This double taxation discourages much-needed investment. Harvard economist Dale Jorgensen calculates that double taxation reduces our national wealth by about a trillion dollars.

Everyone who owns a mutual fund or IRA, or who participates in a 401(k) or typical pension plan, is penalized by this double taxation.

Even relatively low-income Americans increasingly rely on stocks for a portion of their savings. According to the Federal Reserve Bank, from 1989 to 1995 the share of stocks as a percent of total assets doubled for families with incomes under $25,000.

Another classic example of a hidden corporate tax of which the majority of Americans are unaware is the share of payroll taxes supposedly paid for by the employer. Again, to have clarity the taxpayer must be aware of how much he or she is paying in taxes. If the average taxpayer assumes the employer's share of payroll taxes is actually paid by the employer while the opposite is true, clarity is hardly achieved.

According to the government, payroll taxes for Social Security and Medicare are "paid equally by both employees and employers," with each paying 7.65 percent. While that may be true for accounting purposes, economist Walter E. Williams explains how it really works:

> [Y]ou probably already believe . . . that your employer pays half your Social Security. This lie may be demonstrated by pretending that you're my boss. We agree to a wage of $7.00 an hour. You deduct 50 cents an hour as my Social Security contribution and add 50 cents as the "employer contribution," making your cost to hire me $7.50 an hour. My question is: If it cost you $7.50 to hire me, what is my minimum hourly output for you to keep me on the job and stay in business? If you said $7.50 an hour, go to the head of the class, because you also know who pays all of the Social Security tax. The worker does.

Williams's point is this: since the employee is doing the work *for the employer* for which the employer expense is $7.50, it is actually the worker who is paying all the tax. This is the kind of quibbling over semantics usually left to economists, however, so the government is able to get away with maintaining the myth that the employer pays half of Social Security and Medicare. If they actually grasped the truth, the employees might riot in the streets.

The government uses payroll taxes to help finance Social Security and Medicare spending, including Old Age Survivors and Disability Insurance (OASDI) and Hospital Insurance (HI, or Medicare Part A). When the government first imposed these taxes during the 1930s, the rate was a combined 2 percent for earnings up to $3,000 per year. The 1998 combined rate was 15.3 percent: 12.4 percent for OASDI for the first $68,400 of wage income and 2.9 percent for HI for all labor income.

Payroll taxes have increased dramatically since 1937. According to the Institute for Policy Innovation, over 90 percent of American workers pay more in payroll taxes, including the employer's share, than they do in income taxes. Since 1977, the payroll tax rate has grown by nearly one-third, from 11.7 percent to 15.3 percent—and that doesn't include the large increase in the wage base subject to payroll taxes.

A recent Cato Institute study documented the impact that hidden labor taxes have on America's work force. The report found that while an average full-time manufacturing worker earns about $27,200, it costs employers $31,000 to hire the worker due to workers' compensation, unemployment insurance, and the employer's share of Social Security and Medicare taxes. As the study points out, this money could have gone to the employee, or been reinvested by the company. After deducting income and payroll taxes from his paycheck, the worker keeps just $22,400. The total "tax wedge" from labor taxes is $8,600, or 28 percent of the amount the employer pays. The amount rises to 36 percent for employees earning $60,000, nearly half of which does not appear on the pay stub. The average burden imposed by unemployment insurance and workers' compensation taxes is $1,618 per employee.

Since mandated benefits raise the cost of hiring workers, these "benefits" end up destroying jobs and lowering wages. An analysis of federal labor laws, Social Security, and unemployment compensation laws from 1934 to 1940 found that these policies boosted the median unemployment rate from 6.7 percent to 17.2 percent.

The answer to payroll tax madness is something that will be tremendously helpful not only to the economy in general but also to the poor in particular—allowing workers to take a portion of what they would otherwise pay in taxes, invest it in private retirement accounts, and put the rest in their pockets. Additionally, a payroll tax cut is the only cut that liberals cannot complain is only for the rich because it puts money immediately into the wallets of the poor. It empowers the poor in the most basic of ways: it keeps the federal government from stealing their hard-earned money before they even have a chance to put their hands on it. We'll look more closely at private investment accounts in the next chapter.

The Death Tax

You've heard the refrain echoed by the media elites: "The death tax is only paid by the wealthiest 2 percent." The wealthiest 2 percent of what? Of dead people. By whatever name the levy is known—the death tax, estate tax, or inheritance tax—Uncle Sam is taxing people for dying. It's not just stupid and morally wrong; its financially crippling and hurtful to millions of Americans.

As is always the case, the trick to deciphering the 2 percent statistic is understanding how government number-crunchers are doing the math. They're not talking about people with lots of cash stocked away in offshore accounts or people who give annual $10,000 gifts to everyone in the extended family—the maximum before the gift tax kicks in. They're measuring wealth in terms of the value of someone's assets.

The death tax is levied against the government-assessed value of the deceased's property. Rates can begin at 37 percent and rise to as much as 55 percent. In other words, the IRS will reduce the estate left by your parents for you and your siblings by an amount sometimes more than half of the total value. Thus, the legacy left by your parents or left by you to your heirs can be significantly reduced or, depending on liabilities against the estate, even wiped out.

Over 60 percent of Americans die without a will or estate plan in place. This means the estate is divided up according to the impersonal laws of the State. Even with a solid plan, however, the government can take a big bite. The inheritance tax inserts government into families at their most vulnerable time. Wealth and values go hand in hand, and a parent's ability to pass on that wealth is hindered by the confiscating taxes of the government. The passage of assets to one's heirs should be a personal decision, not Uncle Sam's.

The inheritance tax has become an even bigger problem as income and assets rise for many Americans and for those with their own businesses. But its impact against the working poor can be devastating. They have learned that one effective way to avoid death taxes is to spend all of their wealth while alive and then die broke. The death tax encourages behavior that supporters of the tax say they are trying to discourage: leisure, conspicuous consumption, lavish spending, and the early and frequent transmission of wealth to subsequent generations.

Even the death tax on those that are truly rich still hurts the poor. If a large, family-owned steel manufacturer has to lay off workers to pay the death tax in order to keep from having to sell the company, you can't say with a straight face that those laid-off workers haven't been hurt by the death tax. Some careful planning and sharing of assets can usually help one avoid this kind of catastrophe, but not everyone remembers to plan carefully.

Farmers and small businessmen may be quite wealthy in terms of equipment and buildings but have very little cash in the bank. This is because farmers and many small businessmen have to reinvest continually to grow and improve their operations, so they'll have something substantial to pass on to their kids. The death tax crushes those dreams. Farmers who are asset-rich but cash-poor who don't plan carefully for the inevitable may have to sell off their families' legacy just to pay the tax. As CURE noted in a 2001 policy report, 25 percent of black farm owners have had to sell off their farms just to pay the death tax. Sixty-five percent of black farmers in the United States are over the age of sixty-seven, and thanks to the negative reality of the death tax, many of their sons and daughters are getting out of the business.

If you have an image of the death tax being paid only after a rich, old white guy passes, think again. Black-owned businesses more than doubled in number between 1987 and 1997, and income levels of black households tripled in the past twenty-four years. A high percentage of these are family businesses, so due to the financial volatility of most of these as family-owned proprietorships, the death tax will result in more than a million black-owned businesses failing or closing. Black-owned businesses tend to have a much higher number of black and minority employees—all of whom suffer when the business must shut down due to the death tax. Some 90 percent of surveyed minority business owners know that they might be subjected to the federal estate tax, creating a situation where their heirs will not be able to continue in the business.

The great irony in all this is that small business owners are affected more by death taxes than the rich corporations liberals have targeted with this redistribution plan. Major corporations are hardly affected because their ownership is so dispersed. On the other hand, businesses owned by families can be ravaged. The government doesn't care in the least if a business is making a small profit or losing money; if the owner passes, the estate will still have to pay death taxes.

In a 1995 study of how small businesses perceive the estate tax, economists Joseph Astachan and Graig Aronoff found that about 67 percent of the businesses aware of the federal estate tax have taken steps (including gifts of stock, ownership restructuring, life insurance purchases, and buy/sell agreements) to shelter their assets from taxation. Over 50 percent of these same business owners indicated they would not have taken those steps had there been no estate tax. Some 58 percent of all the business owners in the survey for the Family Enterprise

Center of the Coles School of Business at Kennesaw State College anticipated failure or great difficulty surviving financially after paying their estate taxes. What determines who must pay is based on the full value of all the deceased's property. The issue of profit or appreciation is not considered. The death tax has caused many heirs of family-owned businesses an IRS nightmare.

An example of the destructive effects of the death tax on blacks occurred when the family who inherited the famous and historic *Chicago Defender* newspaper was taxed more than $4 million. The family, forced to seek outside investors, was faced with the probability of having to sell the newspaper to pay the bill. According to Alexis Scott, publisher for the *Atlanta Daily World,* "[T]he impact of the estate tax has been particularly damaging to African American newspapers." Then why did the Congressional Black Caucus stand in opposition when the Congress considered repealing the death tax? Apparently some confused souls started believing their own insane rhetoric against the wealthy.

As the number of entrepreneurs grows, the impact of the death tax grows right along with it, causing an increasing amount of damage in poor communities. Small businesses are still the number one creators of new employment, and the at-risk communities in our country need more entrepreneurs. "Getting rid of the death tax will start to create a needed legacy and begin a cycle of wealth building for blacks in this country," says Harry C. Alford, president and CEO of the National Black Chamber of Commerce. Even if the heirs pay the death taxes mandated by the government, the family might continue to struggle in an attempt to keep alive the family business. Recent data from the U.S. Census Bureau showed that 96 percent of black-owned businesses are either sole proprietorships or partnerships. This only further demonstrates the extra-ordinary fragility of the black economic community and the devastating impact of the death tax against those struggling to tap into the American dream.

Rep. J.C. Watts Jr. (R-OK, retired) stated, "The death tax has prevented many African Americans from building wealth by taxing the estate of the deceased at rates that leave family businesses and living relatives in economic despair."

In short, the death tax does irreparable harm to small and family-owned businesses—the very places many of the American poor begin their ascent from poverty. It discourages them from continuing the business, therefore stifling economic growth in their communities. Solomon said in Proverbs, "A good man leaves an inheritance for his children's children" (13:22)—difficult to do when the government requires each American business to pay a penalty upon the death of its owner.

CHOKING ON RED TAPE

Uncle Sam has grown to be such a behemoth that we are a nation choking on red tape. No one feels this more acutely and painfully than small business owners. A form exists for everything from taxes to health codes to employment issues to anything else you can imagine. It forces small businesses to devote more time to paperwork and less time to improving or expanding the business. Big businesses can manage red tape. They just create entire divisions that do nothing but "compliance"—bureaucrat-speak for dealing with paperwork and red tape. They incorporate it as a business cost, which means higher prices for consumers. But this is a luxury that most small businesses can't afford. As a result, the poor suffer, even when the regulations are designed to help them, such as with minimum wage laws.

Wage Laws

Minimum wage is called the "National Black Teen Unemployment Act" by many economists—and with good reason. Forcing businesses to pay more for every employee means that most companies are going to do one of three things: 1) shut down local operations and move production to another country, 2) tighten screening to find workers actually worth the higher minimum wage, or 3) shift money away from hiring people and toward investing in more technology.

Companies like Levi's have shut down their U.S. operations entirely and have moved to Mexico, where labor is cheaper. The workers they laid off weren't rich, and they certainly weren't helped by the combination of a higher minimum wage and stiff corporate income taxes. Even if you're talking about minimum wage jobs in places like The Gap or McDonald's, suburban housewives and their rich kids are going to be more likely to enter the workforce if they have a higher minimum guaranteed. So not only will there be fewer lower-wage jobs, but the minimum wage laws also entice more people to compete for the fewer spots. Again, it's the poor who lose out.

Doing far more damage than minimum wage laws, though, are so-called living wage laws, which are like minimum wages on steroids. In some cities, like the People's Republic of Berkeley, California, they have a living wage in the ten dollars per hour range. Guess what? Businesses will still have to hire people, but they are going to be a lot more strict about whom they hire, requiring more experience and education, and will try to get more work out of every person they hire. In the end, though, they'll hire fewer people, and all the other problems created by a minimum wage are even worse with a living wage. Once again, this is bad liberal policy that hurts the very people it is intended to help.

Another wage law that hurts the poor is the Davis-Bacon Act. At the urging of the labor union movement, Davis-Bacon was passed in 1931 with the intent to protect local, unionized contractors on federal projects from being replaced by non-unionized contractors, who used low-cost itinerant workers, usually southern blacks and immigrants. Middle-class white labor couldn't compete and begged the government to intervene.

Rep. James Davis (R-PA) and Rep. Robert Bacon (R-NY), who once called for limits on immigration from countries "in which the population is not predominantly of the white race," introduced the bill. With blacks the de facto target of this legislation, those with racist tendencies were quick to jump on board. On the floor of the House of Representatives, Rep. William Upshaw (D-GA) said: "You will not think that a southern man is more than human if he smiles over the fact of your reaction to that real problem you are confronted with in any community with a superabundance or large aggregation of Negro labor." Rep. Clayton Allgood (D-AL) complained on the floor of the House about "cheap colored labor" that is "in competition with white labor throughout the country." Others were less obvious about their racism, referring to black labor as "cheap labor" or "cheap imported labor."

Requiring construction companies under contract to the federal government to pay their workers prevailing wage rates and benefits for federally funded construction projects valued at more than $2,000, the law drastically limited opportunities for minority workers to work on government projects. The law also imposed more regulations on companies who contract with the government, including excessive documentation and specific hiring practices.

Consequent to the passage of this law, a "good old boy" network of white contractors closed ranks, making it virtually impossible for the less-skilled black and immigrant workers to get jobs. For as long as there have been unions, unskilled labor has been the enemy, but Davis-Bacon was created by racists to promote white interests with the stamp of the federal government, and as usual does more harm than good. The law effectively hinders amateur workers from gaining work experience and subjects minorities to the whims of bias. It favors skilled and unionized construction workers, disproportionately white, over unskilled non-unionized workers, who are disproportionately black. This especially hurts the poor because while they cannot necessarily compete on skills, they can on price. And so, in addition to the government's blatant violation of the constitutional principle of equal protection under the law, Uncle Sam blunts one more tool of the poor to escape poverty.

Living up to its racist promises, since its inception, Davis-Bacon has led to outright discrimination against minorities in the construction industry. In 1932, one year after enactment, only thirty of the 4,100 workers employed on the Boulder Dam project were African-American. In 1962, local construction unions in Washington D.C. were successful in preventing black electricians from working on the U.S. Capitol's Rayburn House Office Building project. And the abuses are ongoing. In 1996, the Institute for Justice filed a lawsuit on behalf of four minority construction firms, two of which went out of business because of Davis-Bacon, and three public housing resident organizations whose members could not obtain job and training opportunities due to prevailing wage requirements.

According to Congressional Budget Office figures, Davis-Bacon costs taxpayers at least $1.5 billion each year through inflated construction costs. This is primarily because the prevailing wage determinations made by the Department of Labor do not reflect market wages. In Oakland, California, carpenters get about twenty-eight dollars an hour on federally funded projects; the pay in private construction is about fifteen dollars per hour.

Repealing Davis-Bacon would be beneficial for three important reasons. First, this would remove a major impediment to unskilled minority workers entering the construction industry and minority firms competing for contracts. Second, it would allow federal, state, and local construction dollars to go further because costs would be lower and productivity higher. Taxpayers would get more for their money. Third, it would allow free markets, instead of bureaucrats, to determine wages on federally funded construction projects.

A modern Congress would never pass the Davis-Bacon Act because its supporters would be condemned as racists. In 1993, the Institute for

Justice challenged Davis-Bacon by bringing suit against the Department of Labor on the grounds that the law was discriminatory. Unfortunately, efforts to repeal the law have been unsuccessful.

The only group who actively supports keeping Davis-Bacon in its present form is the building and construction trade unions and their allies in Congress. Sometimes the rich and powerful do abuse the poor. They just use government to do it.

Rent Control

Rent control came into being because liberals decided that housing was too expensive and passed laws to set limits on the amount of rent some landlords may charge. In a free market, investment would flow in the direction of housing to meet the demand. If housing demands surpassed the supply, prices would be high. The high price would be temporary, however, because the demand for additional housing would attract more investors to build new housing, and prices would fall. We always hear the cry from liberals that taxpayers should provide "affordable" housing, particularly for the low-wage workers of a community. But what they forget about economics is that entrepreneurs and investors are not inclined to put time, energy, or money into something that will not produce profits, regardless of how noble the cause.

When the government manipulates these profit potentials through rent control laws and other government subsidies, entrepreneurs will reduce their investments in building houses and apartments, and some landlords will find other uses for their properties. As author David Chilton points out in his book, *Productive Christians in an Age of Guilt Manipulators*, Uncle Sam cannot bring supply and demand together.

Price controls will reduce not only the supply of goods but the quality of goods as well. Landlords will try to reduce their costs by cutting down the quality of their housing since there is no market incentive for them to retain high standards. They will not seek to keep up the plumbing facilities and so forth, because with the shortage of housing due to the controlled price, they do not have to compete for renters. They will always be able to find people so desperate for housing that anything will do. So improvements are not made and breakdowns are not repaired.

Chilton's research also concluded that if costs are prohibited and losses are high, many landowners will simply disappear, abandoning their properties altogether, creating even more housing problems than before.

WHAT SHOULD GOVERNMENT DO?

Since the framing of the Constitution, government has shown an ability to do only one thing very well: promoting national defense. At the end of the day, who would argue that government as it exists today has not reached well beyond any perception of necessity envisioned by America's founders? Human nature being what it is, mankind will continue to demonstrate tendencies towards corruption, deceit, and a raft of other evils, but we must develop and promote a mindset that government should be enlarged and empowered only as a last resort. Every opportunity we have to shrink and weaken the power of government—except in the area of national and civil defense—should be pursued.

Some folks would point to Enron as just cause for government control over capitalism and how all people make and spend their money, but once again, personal responsibility is a lesson we would all do well to learn from the Enron scandal. Legislators can look into legal loopholes or market flaws, or grandstand about new government protections and bailouts, but let's face it: Uncle Sam cannot protect us from every crook and fraud. We have to take some personal responsibility for our own actions.

Didn't any of Enron's thousands of employees question his or her skyrocketing stock portfolio amid California's energy collapse? Did not one Enron worker think to read the conditions of his or her 401(k) plan in case the company failed? You don't need an MBA to know that even giant corporations can tank.

Putting our trust in a bloated, inefficient government bureaucracy for everything from healthcare to retirement security may ultimately prove disastrous. If employees had total power and responsibility to create and hone their own benefit plans, maybe workers could avoid future Enron-type disasters by themselves and skip all the federal red tape, not to mention the added benefit of keeping more of their hard-earned money because the government managers would be out of the picture.

Government will never do a good job of managing other people's money; just look at their track record. We need to start asking important questions, like, "What if Social Security was paid out in full over a two year period to Individual Retirement Accounts owned by every individual in the system?" Sure it would create a huge temporary deficit, and the banking industry would have to be monitored for unfair practice and abuse, but so what? Didn't we just spend $70 billion on a war with Iraq? Wouldn't it be worth it if we could dismantle the Social Security Administration in five years? How much money would that save over time? Any politicians out there feel like finding five smooth stones for their slings and taking down a big, ugly giant?

Here's another great question, "If it works for Social Security, would something similar work for Medicare—maybe using healthcare or medical savings accounts?" To borrow an idea from a G. Gordon Liddy broadcast, so much of government social policy is based on the assumption that if you make a fist and sling it at my face, I won't duck. You can bet your bottom dollar most people don't want to end up on the street eating dog food out of a can. Some may end up like that, but let's give incentives to private organizations to help those people and get government out of the social program business.

The market works. We must endeavor on every front possible to get the money out of the government's hands and back into the hands of the people, where it belongs. The era of pork barrel politics must be put behind us. We will always have the judiciary to keep those people inclined to bend the rules in line, but with most regulation, certain taxes, and all bureaucrats out of the equation, the net result should be a thriving, robust economy, and maybe, more important, a streamlined, more efficient federal government. The bright, creative, and remarkable people of this great nation deserve nothing less. And the poor certainly deserve much better than they are getting now.

8

From Entitlement to Empowerment

I hate the word "minority." Not the actual word, mind you, without which we would be hard-pressed to describe small groups not in the majority and would have been forced to watch the Tom Cruise blockbuster, *Small-Group-Not-in-the-Majority Report*. No, I hate the word as it has evolved as a political label. I hate it because it has been weighed down with meaning, until my only associations with it are negative and political. Like the commandeering of the word "gay," which used to mean "happy," when I hear the word "minority" all that comes to mind are exercises in power and manipulation.

There has been much publicity recently about the surge in the number of Hispanic Americans. Numbering almost forty million, Latinos are now the largest minority group in the United States. But, what does that mean? Is minority defined by quantity? It defies logic that a group numbering forty million, a population larger than some countries, should be thought of as a minority. There are a couple million Arab Americans. Are they a minority? There are about five million Jews in the United States. They certainly aren't considered a minority. Clearly, this has nothing to do with population count. So what defines a minority?

In Genesis, God created animals and then directed Adam to give them names. First came the reality, and then came the names. Politics works the other way around. First we create the name, and then we create the reality. This is the perversity of politics. In the process of finally getting rid of the despicable signs over facilities that said "Whites Only" or "Blacks Only," we created a new public trough with a sign over it that says "Minorities Only." Any group that could be qualified as a minority could open the door to a vast array of government programs.

Being a minority seems to imply being uniquely disadvantaged in some way. As with most liberal definitions, however, the truth is something different altogether. Beginning in the 1960s, the United States experienced an influx of non-European immigrants at a time when the idea of rights was becoming totally detached from the notion of responsibility and citizenship. These new groups arriving in the United States experienced the same hardships, discomforts, and lack of acceptance suffered by the Irish, the Italians, the Jews, and the many other groups who arrived in the United States over the last two hundred years. The difference was that these immigrants arrived in an era when rights took on a life of their own—rights for their own sake, no longer imbued by a Creator, but conferred by a liberal government.

This is not intended as any kind of rebuke against the Latinos, Asians, or any other minority community, but merely a warning: Don't be seduced by the government program pusher. Look at what it has done to my black brothers and sisters and learn to solve your own problems as a community.

I know the social struggle of blacks in America resonates with me since I've lived it, but those black Americans who are descendants of slaves really are the ethnic group with the most reason to feel different from the rest of the population. Taken as a group, black Americans are the only Americans whose ancestors did not come to this country by choice. Certainly blacks don't have a lock on discrimination, but I can think of no other group in our country whose ancestors were so widely regarded as less than human upon their arrival. The legacy of slavery and dehumanization and the painful history of segregation, lynching, and discrimination that followed set apart the black psyche in the United States today. Please understand I seek no special rights because of past suffering, and I think talk of reparations is ridiculous to the point of being absurd. Any attempt, however, to address the issues of black America must take into account the fact that because our history is different and unique, our problems today are different and unique. The important question is where do we go from here, and how?

As a woman of faith, I believe events have purpose and meaning. My faith tells me that the Lord gives no man a burden he cannot bear. So, I am an optimist. I believe that, on the issue of race, challenges remain for blacks and whites alike. Meeting these challenges will move our country to a beautiful new chapter in its history.

From the black perspective, we get scripts from the Left and from the Right, and I believe both of these scripts are unacceptable. From the Left, the script says that black Americans are debilitated by their history. This belief produces a fatalism that leads to hopelessness and despair. No daylight shines into the tunnel of poverty. When there does seem to be a ray of light, it is beamed in by a politician who presents himself or herself as the great and essential liberator. The Left defines black reality as a political reality. Without the exercise of political power to fix what is broken, to right what is wrong, blacks will never get a chance in white society.

From the Right, blacks hear that it is time to forget about the past. Get over it and move on. Besides, even though it was a terrible thing for your ancestors to be kidnapped and sold into slavery, has it not turned out to be a blessing in disguise? After all, aren't you a lot better off in the land of opportunity than running around in an African village somewhere? I mean, they don't even have televisions!

So, take the message from the Right and pass it to the Left: forget about the past already. Keep your programs and taxes and social engineering. Stop casting us as victims. You are not our savior. To the Right

I say indeed let's move on, but don't you dare tell me to get over it. Good and bad, our history is our history, and our suffering is our suffering. It is part of who we are, and in time God will use the spade of sorrow to plant joy and heal the brokenhearted. Reconciliation waits in the wings, but our wounds are not as old as you may think. We must be allowed to mourn for as long as it takes, even as we move forward together.

To my black brothers and sisters, I say take the chip off your shoulder and believe that God, providence, or even fate brought you here for a reason, to do a job that no one else can do. For all our painful history, we bring richness and culture to our nation unlike any other group. This is not about politics; this is about faith, freedom, and opportunity. Take up the burden of your destiny and dare to dream. Our greatest fear is not that we won't measure up. Our greatest fear is that we are incredibly unique and wonderful. It is our potential for greatness, not our weakness, that is most frightening to us.

You are a unique individual. There is no one like you. Out of six billion people, you are the only you. You are not in competition with anyone to be yourself. The future you have barely dared to imagine for yourself is yours for the taking. All you have to do is step out and never, never, never give up. If you think all your problems are because of the white man and all your solutions are because of the government man, then who are you? How can you have others believe in you if you don't believe in yourself? Understand that the beginning of freedom is taking personal responsibility.

We have to keep it real. What person does not carry their history around with them? Understanding where we have been is critical to understanding who we are today. To pull black Americans out of their history is no different from having pulled our ancestors out of their homelands. We must know our history without being ruled by it. We have to move beyond "how we got here" to "where we are going." Whether you worship at a church, synagogue, mosque, or YMCA, we have to come together as a community, build bridges instead of walls, dust off our old tools of forgiveness and sacrifice, and work together for our common good. Let us earn the right to complain by sweating blood to bring about change.

The battle will be uphill. The emotional wounds of the slave owner and his descendents do not run as deep. I have heard the founders' capitulation to slavery rationalized in different ways: *Forgive them because they were products of their time. Moses slew the Egyptian taskmaster three thousand years ago. There never would have been agreement on the Union without the acceptance of slavery.*

It does not diminish the greatness of the founders to acknowledge that they were fallible. Acknowledgement of their flaws can bring humility and understanding. Until we can accept the past and stop pointing the finger, it will be difficult to circumvent the tendency to resort to the heavy hand of government to try to right the wrongs. Our success will depend on our ability to reason together and patiently pursue middle ground through the language of compromise. If we solve the problems ourselves, the need for government intervention dissolves.

Despite the brilliance of the founding fathers in crafting the Constitution, one has to wonder about the wisdom of putting our collective fate in the hands of politicians. It reminds me of an email circulating that asked, "Can you imagine working at the following company? It has a little over 500 employees with the following statistics: 29 have been accused of spousal abuse, 7 have been arrested for fraud, 19 have been accused of writing bad checks, 117 have bankrupted at least two businesses, 3 have been arrested for assault, 71 cannot get a credit card due to bad credit, 14 have been arrested on drug-related charges, 8 have been arrested for shoplifting, 21 are current defendants in lawsuits. In 1998 alone, 84 were stopped for drunk driving. Can you guess which organization this is? It's the 535 members of the 108th United States Congress. The same group that perpetually cranks out hundreds upon hundreds of new laws designed to keep the rest of us in line." We're a mob of flawed human beings run by a mob of flawed human beings, and on issues of race and poverty, we desperately need a new game plan.

There are six mission-critical challenges for those interested in responding effectively to race and poverty on Uncle Sam's Plantation:

1. dismantle so-called multiculturalism,
2. abolish affirmative action,
3. abandon the faith-based initiative,
4. personalize welfare services,
5. allow school choice,
6. personalize Social Security.

MYTHS OF MULTICULTURALISM

During the war in Iraq, many of us heard the incredible story of supposed foreign terrorists who rolled grenades into three tents killing a captain and injuring fifteen others, including a brigade commander. Then, to our amazement, we found out that it was one of our own soldiers who had done the deed. How is it that this soldier in one of America's most elite divisions of the army could committ such an atrocity against his fellow servicemen?

The actions of Sgt. Asan Akbar can be explained in one word: *multiculturalism.* Far too many youths have been taught to hate America because they believe the lie that Western culture is evil and Christianity is racist. Young men like Akbar are exposed to years of hating America speech from Louis Farrakhan, Maxine Waters, Cornell West, Cynthia McKinney, and all those other demagogues whose platform is to blame everything that is wrong in this world on the institutions and culture of Western civilization.

I recently read a *National Review Online* article by Dave Kopel of the Independence Institute in which he gave the following excellent, and biting, definition of this overly used and abused word: "'Multi-culturalism' is a code word for putting students in racially segregated dormitories, trashing Western culture, and promoting ignorance of cultures other than one's own. But few dare to object to this racist policy, for fear of being called 'racist' by the Orwellian racists of political correctness."

Technically, the word has a number of definitions ranging from "of many cultures" to "a doctrine or cult, which adheres to the maintenance of many cultures." However, as with many words in the liberal lexicon, "multiculturalism" has gained a wholly different and perverse meaning in the last thirty years thanks to special interest groups and social engineers who wish to see an entirely different cultural and political landscape than the one drawn by our founding fathers.

Our country is one of the most culturally and religiously diverse countries in the world and has been so since its inception. English settlers weren't the only ones to tame the New World. Spanish, French, German, Swedish, Asian, and African immigrants also brought with them talents and gifts that have benefited our nation in a way that cannot be compared with any other. The Irish, one of the most despised groups of the 1800s, became the backbone for much of the U.S. economy. The United States is a many-cultured society. In that sense of the word, our nation has always been multicultural—in fact, one of the most profoundly multicultural societies in the world.

Enter the liberals, offended by our Eurocentric origins and male-dominated Judeo-Christian heritage. Christians say their way is the only way, so they must be silenced. Traditional marriage puts men in control, so it must be weakened. As the strongest nation in the world, America needs to be kept in its place, so all cultures except American culture must be promoted. In their arrogance, liberals believed they were the guardians of truth and equality and everyone else was ignorant of the fact that we were already a pluralistic society. To accomplish their goals, they decided to make it taboo to talk negatively about anyone else's culture—even those things that are manifestly negative in a particular culture, e.g., the way one may be debilitated by superstition or the way another may mistreat women.

This view of multiculturalism demands we not only befriend and accept other cultures but also approve of every aspect of their culture no matter how offensive or immoral. This is important because in redefining multiculturalism liberals have slipped in the idea that we must also accept all forms of morality regardless of how out of step they may be with traditional American culture. Remember, by and large, the Left views morals not as transcendent but rather as subjective—so who can say one behavior is more moral than another?

The danger of the liberal definition of multiculturalism to our society is that it blurs the lines of right and wrong and brings confusion to a once well-ordered society. This form of multiculturalism would like to argue that no one's view of morality and virtue is correct, and, yet, all are correct at the same time. In other words, no one can be right, and no one can be wrong. Now tell me this, how can the head-hunting religions of Malaysia and other areas of southeast Asia be on par with Christianity, a religion in which adherents are expected to love their neighbor as themselves?

While the Left has propagated this idea that everyone is "okay" and there are no absolutes in society, they've also made it abundantly clear that their new form of morality is absolute. Dr. Thomas Oden of Drew University has called it "absolute moral relativism." And they bully others into adopting it. Consequently, decent Americans are forced by political correctness to keep quiet.

Other dangers of this new form of multiculturalism, formerly known as "pluralism," are that it promotes segregation, discrimination, and racism. One need look no further than the recent Supreme Court case regarding affirmative action at the University of Michigan. Rather than promoting equality and fairness based on the content of one's character and achievement, multiculturalism today only sees the color of one's skin, in stark contrast to its self-righteous claims of colorblindness.

This new definition of multiculturalism is faulty in its very premise. It is important to point out that the U.S. is a country that has long protected religious freedom and respected a diversity of cultures. All it has asked is that its citizens hold to certain virtues that are common to all, virtues that have made this country great and cannot be compromised. Multiculturalism, according to the Left, assumes and tries to reinforce the notion that there is no central core of beliefs and virtues to which we all ascribe. This is ridiculous. Regardless of culture, nearly every society holds to the same or similar virtues, such as bravery, fidelity, loyalty, and honesty. C.S. Lewis made this case brilliantly in his book, *The Abolition of Man*. While there may be tribes here and there that place high value on the art of betraying a friend or subscribe to vulgar, violent rituals, there isn't a single culture in the world that awards medals to its soldiers for running away in battle (except, possibly, in France). Even those societies in Africa and the Middle East that believe it is acceptable to have more than one wife hold the moral position that adultery is wrong. And even thieves understand stealing is wrong. Just try stealing from a thief.

The ultimate problem with this notion of multiculturalism is that there must be truth somewhere. There must be a final arbitrator in matters of law and justice. While our federal government is forbidden by the Constitution from promoting any one form of religion, it must hold to some form of truth that is without compromise; otherwise, every form of behavior can be accepted, excused, or justified, under the right circumstances.

The race-baiting demagogues are partially accountable for the situation with Sgt. Asan Akbar. Only time will tell if the American people will excuse his behavior because of his opposition to the war and his tension from being a Muslim. But the fact is there is no explanation which in any way mitigates this man's guilt. He should have been brought before a military tribunal the following day, and if found guilty, he should have been executed immediately.

Akbar was not the first black Muslim soldier to turn on his fellow troops. In November 2002, the *Seattle Times* reported that during the Gulf War in 1991, a soldier by the name of John Allen Muhammad threw a grenade into a tent in which sixteen of his fellow soldiers were housed. Perhaps you recognize that name as the older of the two snipers who terrorized the Washington D.C. area and killed thirteen innocent and unarmed Americans shortly after September 11, 2002. Indeed, they are one and the same. If Muhammad had been given life in prison or executed for his heinous crime, those thirteen people might still be alive.

Multiculturalism in the hands of liberals is more than misguided; it is dangerous. It weakens America at precisely the time we need to be strong; it allows attempted murderers to go free to try to kill again. Make no mistake, if you do anything you can to dismantle multiculturalism, you are a genuine patriot. Let the liberals yell, "Racist!" The cancer must be cut out if we dare aspire to greatness for our country.

AFFIRMATIVE ACTION: END IT—DON'T MEND IT

Harry Belafonte called the Colin Powells of the world "house slaves" because they do not believe that advancements in life rest upon ethnicity or that their skin color is a scarlet letter. This is typical liberal arrogance, disparaging people for the unpardonable sin of disagreeing with them. No, the Powells, Clarence Thomases, Alan Keyeses, and Condi Rices of the world understand that some people, both black and white, simply strive to be good people and morally sensitive to all. The abolishment of affirmative action programs would help reveal whether any good people are in the admissions departments of America's universities and colleges or in the hiring departments of any major corporations and businesses.

Take the system of slavery as an example. Slavery was legal, but not everybody who could afford to own a slave bought one. In fact, some vehemently opposed it at great personal risk. Now, I know Dr. Claud Anderson implied in his book, *Black Labor, White Wealth,* that all whites were guilty participants in slavery by virtue of buying cotton, but failure to organize a boycott is a far cry from guilty participation. Unless we are prepared to stop driving on that highway built by lottery money—knowing how gambling destroys lives—or stop buying gasoline because some of the money ends up supporting terrorists, we had better not head down that road.

Too much of the affirmative action debate, however, is focused on whether it is a fair system, or a quota system. Why are liberals like Al Sharpton not willing to let the New Jersey state troopers use racial profiles to combat crime yet are willing to demand racial profiling to secure admission to certain universities? Why did the three students rejected by the University of Michigan target the twenty-point bonus given to minorities in their lawsuit and not the twenty points set aside for the children of alumni? The ugly fact of affirmative action is that blacks feel that they are going to be discriminated against if the choice comes down between them and an equally qualified white applicant, while whites feel that for every black chosen a white is being displaced.

The success of blacks in education or commerce should not result from a program but from the fact that they were willing to make the effort to excel. That means performing well enough in high school and on their SATs to be admitted to the college of their choice or to pursue the job of their choice. Black students are not wired to be slothful any more than Asians are wired to be studious or Irish are wired to like corned beef and cabbage—but these behaviors are conditioned through culture. This conditioning usually comes from parents, particularly the father in the home, which is why the rate of family breakdown in the black community is a great detriment to black achievement. The pretense of equality through quotas is a façade. Equality will never result from a system of coercion with promotions based on ethnicity instead of work ethic.

On the other hand, many conservatives have taken a "colorblind" position that is just as extreme as a quota system. Attempts to ignore the obvious are ridiculous. Just the other day, a blond-haired, blue-eyed five-year-old asked me, "Why are you brown all over?" This was not the first time I've been asked this by an innocent child. My first thought was to jokingly ask, "How do you know that my butt is brown?" But due to his age I told him, "God loved coloring the rainbow and the flowers so much that he decided to make people different colors too." (I wanted to add, "When after making only four colors of people, He had to break up so many fights He decided not to keep going, before we destroyed the rest of His creation," but I left well enough alone.)

Pretending to be colorblind will not heal the cultural divide that exists in our nation. Mainly because the cultural divide is just that, a cultural divide, as opposed to being only a color divide. One factor that has facilitated the cultural divide is the blurring of the terms culture and ethnicity. These two words are not synonymous. One's ethnicity has to do with race or a mixture of racial heritage in the lineage. This is quite different from one's culture. Culture comes from the things you have in common with other people regardless of their ethnic background. Although a common ethnicity or skin color can be a part of one's culture, it is never the only element that defines a culture. They are the customs and traditions, combined with the laws, beliefs, language, and art, which provide the major components. When held in common by a group, these defining factors become a culture.

While one's ethnicity can be diluted, it cannot be lost. However, the same is not true with culture. When someone says "back in our day" or "in today's world," what is being acknowledged is a change or loss of some aspect of culture. Also revealed in those statements is the loss of something else a culture holds in common—a worldview. As culture changes, so does the way society sees the world. It is in that cultural worldview that we formulate the responsibility of the members of society, both personally and corporately.

The cultural divide as it exists in America today is due to a lack of common culture, not a lack of common ethnicity. For this reason, neither pretense nor quotas will ever heal the cultural divide. Because of the ethnic diversity found in America, the experience of genuine community can only come from a common culture that transcends ethnicity and diversity.

The Judeo-Christian culture upon which America was founded met that requirement for those who chose to come to this new land of promise in search of a better life. The Judeo-Christian culture provided the ethic that gave us a common law that transcended the cultural backgrounds of the various pilgrims coming to these shores. Have you ever considered the cultural differences of the original pilgrims and every immigrant group since? You do not have to look very far to discover culturally and ethnically diverse settlements, but when you examine the fabric of the nation, it was the absolutism of Christian culture that provided a common thread sufficient to weave together even those with diverse religious distinctions. When the common thread of this culture began unraveling, society experienced a void. Left with only the limited parameters of reasoning, society began to fill that void with relativistic theories like multiculturalism and its end result in terms of public policy: affirmative action.

Culture is critical to our lives because no man is an island. Individuals cannot thrive in a vacuum. The twentieth century left us uprooted from the deepest and strongest supports of life, our communities of family and faith. With structure and common culture stripped away, life loses its great meaning, strength, and high purpose. Without a common culture, people find themselves autonomous and disconnected from the fellowship of community. We would rather shop online than deal with people at the mall. Most suburban residents enter their garage from their house, get in their car, click the door-opener to raise the garage door, and wave at their neighbors from the privacy of their car as they drive away. In *The Great Divorce*, C.S. Lewis envisioned a version of hell where people could create real estate with a thought, so of course, everyone lived a hundred miles away from everyone else.

If we are serious about helping people move from an entitlement culture of affirmative action to an empowerment culture or individual merit, then we have to reestablish a common culture of rules and ethics. People need a solid framework upon which to build their lives. A person cannot depend upon his own self as the sole source to determine right, wrong, rules, and values, or we are all in deep trouble.

EXERCISE REAL FAITH: DITCH THE FAITH-BASED INITIATIVE

The faith-based initiative is our latest proof that politicians are great entrepreneurs when it comes to finding ways to expand the scope of government, their own power, and control over our lives. This particular initiative goes in the opposite direction from the intentions of the Charitable Choice provision in the welfare bill and should be of concern to all because, in the best scenario, it will only waste money. In the worst case, however, it will destroy our nation.

The Charitable Choice provision in the federal welfare bill allowed charities to focus on caring for those in need of help without having to answer to several layers of bureaucracy or testy politicians. It gutted some burdensome rules and streamlined outdated procedures in order to slash the regulations and red tape for nonprofit organizations. Charitable Choice also required that states that contract out welfare services to the private sector not discriminate against private charities even if they are religious. That type of discrimination in selective welfare service providers had created a wedge between the public and private organizations that assist the poor. Only secular programs qualified to bid on state contracts for welfare services, which shut out most of the effective programs. Charitable Choice removed this barrier. The faith-based initiative creates new barriers.

Although for President Bush this initiative is a crusade to reach minorities, welfare programs have already done enough damage in black America. We have demonstrated how government dependency has created an environment in which black illegitimacy rates have soared. This time the victim of government intervention will be the black church. Those who claim that the faith-based initiative merely saves charitable programs of religious organizations from discrimination miss the most basic point. The main reason faith-based programs are successful is the fact that free people choose to fund them and free people choose to participate in them. The government needs to get out of the business of social programs, and the religious community needs to dust off its traditional role and fill that void.

There are four reasons faith-based service providers should oppose all proposals of direct federal aid to any private charity group:

1. Evangelism. You cannot gut proselytizing from religious-run programs, as Bush's plan does, and expect them to work. These programs work precisely because the workers are free to discipline and disciple. The most successful of these programs are those that incorporate their religion throughout the curriculum of the program to directly influence attitudes and improve decision-making skills. The direct grant proposal to control the religious personality of qualifying charities is government censorship of religion. This preferential treatment towards nonsectarian religious groups not only borders on violating the establishment clause of the Constitution but also marginalizes nontraditional service providers.

2. *Competition.* The competitive edge a government grant would give to its preferred, non-proselytizing charities would minimize the availability and variety of non-government-funded charity services, thus limiting service options for the needy. Most small conservative charities serving the hardest hit at-risk communities will never apply for a government grant yet will be forced to compete with government-endowed charities. The monopolistic effect of government will inevitably force smaller charities out of business. (In addition, there is already evidence that the assistance offered by many of the non-proselytizing charities includes abortion services, entitlement philosophies, and other things ideologically at odds with many taxpayers.)

3. *Dependency.* Most Americans agree that government welfare programs create a cycle of dependency. The expansion of existing welfare programs to include more churches and other faith-based service providers would increase dependency on government to solve the problems of the needy. When people lose the satisfaction resulting from the sacrifice of volunteering time and money to work with the needy, the charity loses the heart of the volunteer. Being compassionate with other people's money will destroy the spirit of true charity. The inevitable loss of this personal touch and commitment will reduce the individual in need to the level of a broken product needing a technical answer or scientific solution to be repaired.

4. *Big Brother.* The amount of red tape necessary to ensure that government-preferred charities are not proselytizing is expensive and complicated. New government tracking laws will put Uncle Sam in a position to set the rules for what qualifies as religious and what does not. This expansion of government regulatory authority will be costly and intrusive. Lawsuits brought on by civil liberty organizations against

charities that supposedly blur the faith-based non-proselytizing rules will also increase the legal burdens of these charities as well as the courts. The bottom line is Charitable Choice should not mean the government's choice.

The truth is we all are already participating in a great faith-based initiative. It is called the United States of America, and its principles and rules are in the Declaration of Independence and the Constitution. When we examine these great documents, we see that the founders referenced our most fundamental rights to our Creator and then defined the role of government to secure these rights. Our great and blessed country has been a story of unprecedented success because of the crucial premise that man is and must be free to exercise his God-given rights.

It is worth noting that although the founders declared this, they prohibited, in the very first amendment to the Constitution, the establishment of religion by government. Clearly, they did not make haste to keep government out of religion because they were not religious men or because they were opposed to religion or religious activity. They did this because they understood that theocracies are rarely free, that faith, freedom, and choice cannot be separated, and that it is critical to preserve and protect these core elements of our society. Our goal should be to eliminate government from those aspects of our society that have been unwisely politicized, not to politicize the very faiths and freedoms that have made our country great. The very idea of welfare is the antithesis of both faith and freedom. And let's be honest: the government makes a lousy board member for any organization.

A true faith-based initiative is one defined by freedom and not by politics. Humankind already has a tragic history of incidents where governments and politicians have gotten into the business of defining faith and religion. Can you say *Crusades?*

Let Congress return the billions of dollars in our welfare budgets to our citizens and have faith they will make the right decisions regarding charitable giving. Let us remember the simple wisdom of Ronald Reagan: that often government is the problem, not the solution.

WELFARE WITH A MORE PERSONAL TOUCH

Given that the faith-based initiative has been under heavy fire from both sides of the political fence, President George W. Bush needs alternative solutions to further reform welfare. The goal of government post-1996 welfare reform should be to get out of the charity business. At some point, society must admit that political programs cannot appropriately assist people in need because need is a moral judgment. That is why the work of charity must be conducted by the private sector. Need, whatever that need might be, is a private matter, often with personal and intimate complexities. Ideally, politicians should be looking for ways to dismantle the existing government programs leaving only the question of what should be done to transition those already on welfare.

Churches and religious groups should be a part of the social services fabric, but direct grants to those organizations are not the answer.

To solve the problem of moving current welfare recipients away from government dependency, I propose that President Bush enact a two-pronged strategy consisting of charitable empowerment zones and vouchers. This truly innovative approach would utilize market-based forces to implement a successful and constitutional approach to charitable choice. How would charitable empowerment zones work? Thanks to work already done with economic empowerment zones, the federal government is already tracking those urban and rural areas in greatest need and can designate these areas accordingly. Congress would then pass a bill granting charitable tax credits for donations to charities located in or providing services within the specified zones. These zones would be selected by demographic data specifying the crime and poverty status of the community. The Department of Justice and HUD would provide a directory of all existing charities in these zones by zip codes and state, which the post office could mail as needed. The directory could list specific information about each charity and its mission.

The legislature would allow annual charitable tax credits up to $1,000 for individuals and $10,000 for corporations for donations to one specific charity in an at-risk community. Resources would flow directly to groups working in the most needy neighborhoods. Charitable empowerment zones would avoid many of the thorny issues of the current faith-based initiative. The Achilles heel of the president's plan is the prospect of direct grants to religious groups and subsequent government control. Rev. Pat Robertson has pointed out the perils of giving money to such groups as the Church of Scientology or the Unification Church, but his solution of the government creating a list and checking it twice is simply a bad idea. Inevitably, politicians and bureaucrats would pick winners and losers, favoring "preferred" groups or religions, and the program would get bogged down in a morass of infighting.

In 2002, Robertson's organization, Operation Blessing, received a $500,000 government welfare grant, and since then, we haven't heard disagreement from him on this issue. In a liberal White House, however, Rev. Robertson's charities could be taken off the list. Throughout the years, the Supreme Court has only approved limited direct funding to religious schools, for example, usually restricted to buying secular textbooks and equipment. Giving large sums of money to thousands of churches and religious groups nationwide is very different from buying books or computers for a local private school.

With appropriate accountability, the constitutionality of Bush's program would never be in question, for the people would give money directly to the recognized charity of their choice located within a charitable empowerment zone.

Hand in hand with the charitable empowerment zones would be a system of vouchers. The welfare recipient would receive a voucher—usable only by the recipient—to redeem for whatever training or assistance programs they are required to receive. The welfare recipient would then take the vouchers to the charities of their choice, whether for housing, daycare, parenting courses, etiquette or job training, anger management, marriage counseling, conflict resolution, domestic mediation, drug rehabilitation, or maternity services. This would minimize direct government contact with the service providers, and money would flow through the voucher recipients. Government could not play favorites; only the people seeking services would.

In order for vouchers to be effective, government would need to get out of the way. The need for micromanaging or mountains of red tape should disappear because the free market would provide all necessary regulation. Ineffective programs or programs that can't deliver services at a reasonable cost will simply shut down because people will stop patronizing them once the bad word-of-mouth gets out. Unfortunately, government rarely has the impulse to trust people and markets.

Uncle Sam must shut down its poverty plantation. Building Bush's faith-based initiative on charitable empowerment zones and vouchers may be not only smart policy but also a political necessity if we are to gracefully move from entitlement programs to empowering individuals.

CHOICE IN EDUCATION

A good friend told me a story about a cat he and his roommates had in college. He said they would leave an opening in the window, so the cat could come and go as she pleased. She would disappear at her inclination into the big, wide world, embark on her kitty adventures, and then return to the warmth and security of their student apartment. Periodically they would find remnants of those adventures on the living room floor in the form of a bird carcass. Other evidence of those adventures also became clear as the cat began to grow, clearly carrying a new litter of kittens to bring into their apartment and, subsequently, the world at large.

The cat gave birth in great feminist style, needing neither father, nor midwife, nor obstetrician. The midnight adventuress, huntress, and seductress was now a mother. Her owner watched her sprawled out on the floor, purring and soporific, as her tiny offspring nursed, fought, and bounced with boundless energy over her and on each other. As he watched, it occurred to him that the tiny kittens and the quiescent mother, though inhabiting different stages of the cat life cycle, existed in very different realities.

These energetic, cute little kittens couldn't possibly imagine that one day they would be like the fat, tired, and content mother. How could they know that one day they would be almost entirely different creatures, with different needs and desires? Instincts seem to do quite well for cats, acting as an automatic pilot navigating them through all nine lives like clockwork, assuming clockwork includes falling off the television in the middle of a nap. Things are not quite so simple for humans, however. Thanks to free will and more profound self-awareness, our lives are so much more complicated, and we need other mechanisms to process the information we need to live our lives. Core truths need to be transmitted to children in the process we call education, which serves as a guiding source of knowledge and wisdom throughout our lives. We transmit this body of knowledge a hundred ways—in word, in deed, in our churches, in our classrooms—so our children will behave as if they were raised by human beings and not by wolves.

We see every day the results of children turned out into the world without adequate education from parents or schools. Without wisdom from their forebears, and not having the benefits of the ingrained instincts of a cat, these children proceed into the world having little or no foresight and therefore head, sadly and predictably, down a path in which only luck alone can save them from at best a wasted life and, at worst, utter destruction.

According to surveys, the United States is the most religious country in the West. We have more citizens stating belief in God and going regularly to institutions of worship than in Europe. Nevertheless, the Bible is taken lightly in our public life, and it is often considered off limits. In our public schools, the place where most children are educated, Bible study and prayer are not permitted. Whatever rights students have must often be vigorously fought for, sometimes with litigation from religious-rights groups.

Of course, the whole point of the First Amendment was to prevent such struggles from becoming necessary. But today the wide interpretation of the Bill of Rights runs something like this: Our public schools must be free of religion because they are public, and public life in the United States must be consistent with the First Amendment of the Constitution, which prohibits government establishment of religion. The First Amendment is crucial to the freedom which we value in this country. It ensures freedom of religious practice and guarantees against religious discrimination. In this sense, we may say that on the question of religion, the government and public life are neutral. Therefore, our public schools (i.e., our government schools) must be neutral on the question of religion.

This needs rethinking. Not the part about freedom, but the part about neutrality. I would maintain that the claim of neutrality is both deceptive and dangerous. Wherever and whenever a person has a choice, claims of neutrality are bogus. The First Amendment itself reflects a value: the importance of freedom of choice among our citizens regarding religion. It could be otherwise. We choose to structure our free society in this fashion because it reflects our concept of the nature of freedom and the truth it manifests regarding the human condition. This is not neutrality. This is a specific point of view.

Such is the case with education. There is no such thing as a value-free education. The material conveyed to students in the course of a school day is carefully selected. These choices reflect values. What does it mean to be educated? What should an adult citizen know? I believe we have a general consensus that students should learn to read and that they should learn mathematics. However, can we assume education should also include instruction, or at least discussion, on why we learn these things and what ends we choose to pursue with them? Can we really believe it is possible to have an educational system where tools and techniques are conveyed to students without ever discussing why?

Utilitarian objectives are values, too. There was a time when we could conclude that it was important to teach skills so that children could enter the workforce and earn a living to support their families. However, to discuss the idea of family today, in any objective sense, is off limits. It is important to understand that this is not a value-free environment. This is an environment where one set of values has been insidiously displaced by another set. This set of values is permissible to teach because we don't call it religion.

I believe the condition and parameters of our public school system is not only destructive but also unconstitutional. We should appreciate that we are forcing our children into a system that essentially teaches an implicit, and often explicit, set of values, which can easily be called dogma, and families have no way to opt out of this system, unless they can afford private school or have the time and resources to home school. If education continues to be mandatory in our country, we must develop a means of allowing choice. The manner in which we do this, whether through vouchers, tax credits, or scholarship funds, is of less immediate concern to me than the aggressive implementation of programs that allow parents to choose where they send their children to school.

Again, to understand the current reality is to understand that a value-free environment is impossible to achieve. Every school curriculum and program is driven by some kind of values. What makes this particularly destructive is that the children who are captives of this are led to believe that what they are taught is objective.

It is easy to point to problems here in, say, sex-ed classes, but any discussion of history, philosophy, sociology, and just about any other major field of study will at some point have to include the hard questions about God and religion—basic issues of ultimate standards of truth—or the discussion will be incomplete. Try discussing the burning of a black church without mentioning God or religion. What do you get? A news report, maybe, but certainly not anything close to the whole picture. Forget the pastor who served faithfully in the pulpit for forty years, helping control the gang problem by getting kids off the street. Forget about the people in the neighborhood who rallied around the church and helped them rebuild. Forget about the thousands of faithful of every skin color who sent their prayers and gifts and good wishes. Forget all that. A black church burned. Racism lives. Newspapers are sold and programs watched, but never is the whole story told, except sometimes on the Fox News Channel. The liberals and their lap dogs in the media should hang their heads in shame.

Since there can be no proof God does not exist, atheism is merely a belief system too. So are multiculturalism and liberalism. All of these by proclamation or inference enthrone man as God, as the ultimate authority. If man is God, we are in trouble. If we could all acknowledge the fact that God may exist, maybe we wouldn't be so averse to putting the Ten Commandments or something like them on courtroom or classroom walls. When religion is prohibited, it is not replaced with neutrality. It is replaced with a culture and dogma of meaninglessness that provides neither the discipline nor the love children need to become healthy adults.

Our country needs to be free, but not value-free. I don't want to force my views on my neighbor. What I do want, and what is essential for the future of our country, is the freedom for my neighbor and me to choose where to send our children to school, and for our children to learn there is such a thing as right and wrong.

REAL SOCIAL SECURITY

If ever there was a perfect political issue that could empower minorities to break the cycle of poverty, it is personalizing Social Security. However, it's hard to say whether this type of empowerment will happen without a revolution because sitting at the core of the Social Security debate is paternalism on both sides of the aisle. No one will admit this, of course, but their implicit assumption that the working poor will not or cannot take care of themselves is paternalism disguised as compassion.

Every employed man and woman in America pays a 12.4 percent Social Security tax on earnings up to $84,000, except politicians, most government workers, and the clergy. You don't need to be a CPA to understand that for someone earning $20,000 the $2,480 going into Social Security makes it practically impossible to save any additional money for retirement. As income levels increase, more funds become available for investment in IRAs and 401(k) plans, but few working poor, who are disproportionately nonwhite, will ever reach the $76,000 threshold at which Social Security ceases.

Let's say our worker earning $20,000 is a thirty-five-year-old black man named Joe. Because payroll taxes consume all the money he could possibly save for retirement, Joe is dependent on Social Security. He has no pride of ownership, no sense that he is building a nest egg for his family's future, and no sense of responsibility or control over the fruits of his labor. Joe can only hope that government will take care of him tomorrow if he does what he's told to do today. This is what passes for morality in the nanny State.

As a low-income black male, Joe's life expectancy is roughly sixty-five. Unless he defies the averages, he won't see the magic age of sixty-seven when the government is supposed to start delivering on its promises. Because he owns nothing, Joe will have nothing to pass on to his heirs. Assuming God is good to him and he lives a long life well past sixty-seven, he will collect a monthly retirement check from Social Security of about $1,200.

Now suppose that Joe had invested 12.4 percent of his pay in his own retirement account. According to the Cato Institute, even a low-risk investment—70 percent in a bond fund, 30 percent in a stock index fund—would give him sufficient savings at retirement to provide a monthly payout of $2,400, or twice what Social Security promises to pay.

Simple investment arithmetic demonstrates that Social Security is hurting the poor instead of helping them. So why is it so hard to change the system? For starters, you can't pay everyone out without bankrupting the system. People have been putting money into the system for decades, and they want a chance to get it back. The figures for people at the poverty level, however, turn this into an issue with racial overtones.

According to the Federal Reserve, 49 percent of white families own retirement accounts but only 31 percent of nonwhite families do. As middle-income Americans accumulated wealth in these retirement plans during the boom of the last twenty years, the working poor continued to pay the few dollars they could have saved into Social Security. That helps explain media hand-wringing over the growing wealth gap between rich and poor. Federal Reserve data shows that in 1998 the median net worth of white families was $95,000 compared with $16,000 for black families. In fairness, these numbers need to be understood in the context that white families outnumber black families three to one, and the number for whites includes billionaires like Bill Gates. Still, the gap is considerable.

As a former welfare mother, I understand the devastating effects of government dependency. As a current employer, I understand the harmful effects of the payroll tax on small business owners and the self-employed. Rev. Jesse Jackson once said, "Capitalism without the capital is just an ism." Well, Mr. Jackson, the 12.4 percent Social Security tax being levied against poor people is pushing them closer to another "ism"—pauperism.

As mentioned in the previous chapter, Social Security taxes make it impossible for low-income workers to heed the proverb, "A good man leaves an inheritance for his children's children." Let's release the poor man from this burden. Personal retirement accounts are true reparations for him. The sooner we throw off the paternalistic, business-as-usual lethargy hanging over Social Security in the body politic, the sooner change will come. Politicians will have to decide it is worth the risk of political suicide to tackle the problem head on. It will take some miracles of accounting and personal sacrifice, but the Social Security system must be dismantled.

The road ahead will be difficult. People—and you know who you are—will have to use whatever power, whatever forum, whatever talents they can bring to bear on moving this agenda forward.

If we genuinely want to help the poor move from entitlement to empowerment, we must get past the racial hang-ups that debilitate us and the government programs that block economic growth and independence. These mission-critical challenges—dismantling multiculturalism, abolishing affirmative action, abandoning the faith-based initiative, personalizing welfare services, allowing school choice, and personalizing Social Security—must become the focus of discussions in government, churches, and political caucuses if we are serious about cutting the tendrils that trap Americans in poverty.

9

The Hope of the Poor

It was 4:00 P.M., April 3, 1992, in Los Angeles, and the skyline looked as if some foreign enemy had been dropping bombs. The smoke that filled the air darkened the sun while flames from nearby buildings lit the sky. Looters and angry mobs had taken to the streets of the city in response to the acquittal of four police officers accused of beating motorist Rodney King. My immediate reaction was to adjourn the meeting I was conducting at my office and go find my kids. Angel, then twelve, was at dance class, and a friend was watching Rachel, then two.

"Stay down," I kept yelling at them as I maneuvered to dodge the stray bullets being shot at fire trucks and police cars on the streets. Our neighborhood was ablaze with tension, bullets, and fire. I was determined to get them to safety, but at that moment I didn't know where that might be. The National Guard had set up tanks at our local grocery store and was trying to close down the streets. The streetlights and traffic lights were no longer working. The Korean merchants had barricaded their stores and moved to the rooftops armed with rifles in an attempt to protect their property. Navigating my car became even more difficult as crowds filled the streets, screaming, stealing, running, shooting, and setting more fires. Babies were crying, sirens were blaring, and the city was being left in ashes. I knew I had to get my kids out of there.

Shortly after getting on the 5 Freeway heading south, a calm silence filled the car. Looking out the windows we could see Los Angeles aglow to the east and soon to the south of us. A spirit of lawlessness was consuming the buildings and the people. Glancing in the rearview mirror I could not help but think of Sodom and Gomorrah, so I stopped looking back.

"Where are we going, Mommy," Angel quietly asked. "To Dan and Jackie's. You and Rachel will stay with them a few days until this mess sorts out."

Dan and Jackie are one of the couples at the local church I now attend. They had a custom of opening their home to travelers who visited the church. They looked like matured hippies. Dan's hair was blond and to the middle of his back. Jackie parted her long blond hair in the middle, and she always wore pastel, lacy, flowing dresses. I met them about a year earlier. We had stayed overnight in their home twice before while attending a church conference in South Orange County, California. They had two boys and a girl that they would inconvenience to let us, complete strangers, spend the night. Culturally, blacks did this all the time but rarely across racial lines. I had never known whites who did it.

The situation felt weird to me and caused me to feel uneasy staying in their home, but this time it was an emergency situation. I didn't have time to think about the inconvenience we would cause. Nor could I dwell on the fact that I would be leaving my two young daughters for an uncertain amount of time in an all-white town with people I barely knew. But I had nowhere else to take them. Everyone I knew and trusted lived in Los Angeles. Like me, they were probably scrambling for an opportunity that would offer safety for their children.

I was glad that Dan and Jackie were willing to make room for Angel and Rachel. Once my children were safe, I went back to L.A. to do what I could to protect our property and to look after what was left of my business. Three days later, the riots ended. Neither our home nor my office building had been destroyed. It was safe for my kids to come home.

Upon returning to pick up my kids, Jackie told me that Bishop Randy Adler wanted to see me. She insisted I contact him before I left San Clemente. "Why does the archbishop want to see me?" I wondered. I really admired the bishop and the members of his parish. They had come into Los Angeles a few years earlier to protest at one of the clinics where I had an abortion. The church I attended in L.A. joined with them in several of the protests. I visited their church on a few occasions, especially during the pro-life protests organized by Operation Rescue. My family had also stayed in his home once overnight. But what would he want to see me about now?

"Your entire neighborhood has burned. Your business is ruined. Your church has closed. I really believe the Lord would have you move down here to recover and get new direction." That was all he said when I talked to him.

Me, a black ex-street hustler and ex-welfare con from Los Angeles move behind the "Orange Curtain" into South Orange County, California? A county where one could go an entire week without seeing one African-American? Home of Richard Nixon? A county where every town was Republican-controlled? Was the Bishop crazy? Was he blind? Perhaps he had not noticed that his entire congregation was white. Or did he think me a hermit, or maybe a masochist?

By this point I was a Republican. I had even gained some public recognition as a conservative activist, but Los Angeles was my comfort zone. I love black culture and couldn't imagine living without loud neighbors, gospel music, and soul food stewing next door. In spite of all its problems, there is an excitement about city life. Besides, I hadn't lived in a white neighborhood since childhood, and the memories were awful. And what about school for my kids? I had attended predominately white schools, and they were found wanting. After two months of struggling to reconcile these questions and cultural fears, we moved.

Amazingly, it was a white family that had moved from Texas and become part of this local church who helped us settle into a little house next door to them. It was awkward at first, but our two-year-old daughters seemed to enjoy each other's company. The church enrolled my older daughter into their junior high school. The ladies in the church daycare watched both my girls as I commuted an hour and a half to Los Angeles attempting to nurture my floundering business.

I looked regularly for racism but was constantly greeted with smiles and friendships instead. When I could not recover my business—too many of my advertisers had been burned out by the riots—my new church friends encouraged my transition into radio. They became part of our life and were always there when we were in need. When my marriage dissolved, they nourished me back to wholeness. They helped me take care of my children. Under their care and the safety of their covenant, community concerns calmed down, and within five years I was able to fully pay my own way. I felt so welcomed and comfortable in my new environment. Most evenings I would watch the sun set over the breathtaking Pacific Ocean and dream of staying there forever.

Always at the back of my mind, though, were thoughts of how to take my experiences back into the neighborhood I had left, where the people needed it most. How could I tell those enslaved to welfare that if they would help themselves others would assist? How could I help the suburban Church and the urban Church work together to make my experience a reality for others lost in despair? Could whites and blacks ever unite to restore hope to the poor?

Our nation is at a crossroads. Americans now know that poverty is not an engineering or genetic problem. All of our welfare programs are morally bankrupt and socially and fiscally destructive. People of religious faith could assume a leadership role in replacing the government and truly help. The Church understands salvation, forgiveness, repentance, and restoration. Faith in the good news of the Gospel opens the belief that God is not mad at Anna, my ex-housekeeper who is burdened by fornication. He is not mad at Isabella, the Peruvian servant who is surrounded by sickness, disease, and poverty. He is not mad at my sister Avis who worries to the point of tears that, as a divorced mother, her paychecks will never be enough. Nor is He mad at my friend Marilyn or her daughter who was diagnosed with AIDS. If those who held the keys to moral truths unified and responded to the needy like that small congregation responded to me, there would be no lack of help.

The possibility of a covenant community answers that question of Paul Johnson's, whether altruism and ambition can coexist in America. However, it raises two deeper questions about our commitment to the needy without Uncle Sam. Urban and suburban churches are worlds apart. Some with lack, some with plenty, some fighting crime, poverty, and racism, others fighting homosexual perversion and abortion, and most acting as though they have no kinship with the other. The question of conduct has always preceded government intrusion into private affairs.

I have watched my friends Mike and Joni take care of the three related children they adopted alongside their own daughter for the past five years. They adopted all three because the government was going to separate them. Their concern was that if men and women of faith won't love and nurture orphans, who will? When you think of the sacrifice and investment it takes to raise children, adoption is the essence of "lending to the Lord." Two new boys have joined their family since. The question of challenge to transcend the racial divide in this country is what keeps most of us in our comfort zones. It is easier to wait until problems hit us directly than to seek them out.

It takes personal effort not to stereotype or pre-judge; thus it is an act of volunteerism. Volunteer work can be hard and disruptive. Overcoming racism and discrimination, both externally and in our own personality, and choosing to make a difference is a matter of personal will and not governmental force. That is why all governmental attempts to legislate volunteerism are futile, but the government does not have a monopoly on bureaucratic behavior. People also run churches so there will always be obstacles to be cleared. Unnecessary administrative complexities can limit options for the poor with "my way or the highway" doctrines and divisions. Denominational differences and turf struggles not only confuse those seeking help but also leave Uncle Sam to arbitrate or mediate or control. The Church will be either prophetic or pathetic in its response to the poor. The harvest is plentiful, but it seems the workers are few.

In an article I wrote for *USA Today,* I discussed why local churches should be involved in welfare reform. I argued that a message of faith and work was key to helping women leave welfare. I wrote that it is difficult for a person in crisis to comprehend the moral obligation of personal responsibility without God. How does one understand obligations without a moral commitment? I heard from a number of enraged atheists upon the publishing of the article who were offended at my recommendation. Several suggested that these women would be better served by a life of chance than by being "indoctrinated" with religion. The problem with this worldview is that chance leads people to substitute luck for hope, and when their luck runs out, they have nowhere to turn but to the government. A mindset of chance produces wishing instead of faith. A wish is a longing, a craving, a want. Wishing is born out of the gambler's mentality that could drive one to accumulate debt to make the wish come true. Debt is slavery, and slaves are poor.

Rather than discouraging the poor from becoming a slave to debt, middle-class America leads the debt craze. A wallet full of credit cards has become a status symbol. Some actually feel a sense of pride when the credit card company gives them a "good boy" pat on the back and extends their debt potential a few thousand dollars. Wouldn't it be hypocritical of me to point a finger at someone like Madonna for being a negative role model for having a baby outside of wedlock while pulling out one of many credit cards when I know I can't pay it off at the end of the month?

When he cannot meet the 22 percent interest that he obligated himself to pay, the debt slave prefers that the Department of Commerce police capitalism, manipulate markets, minimize competition, and force lenders to redistribute their wealth on behalf of him and other debt slaves. Instead of personal restraints, the debt slave turns his anger towards free enterprise and the money-lending institutions that bail him out of the consequences of his self-imposed slavery. What the poor need to understand about debt is that lenders and borrowers place different values on money. That is why their habits are different. Lenders are frugal and very conservative in their financial decisions. Borrowers are anxious and financially liberal. Borrowers value money to acquire things. Lenders value money as a negotiation instrument to access dreams; they understand how to ensure the success of their investments. Financial stewardship is critical if one is to move up from poverty.

The fact is that poverty is not inevitable. You can work your way out. "Work my way out?" Yep, faith without works is dead. Living free from poverty is hard work and requires faith. That's one reason secularism is so popular. It is much easier to sit around and wish for something while the government makes promises to bail you out. Faith is simply the action that energizes your beliefs. Every belief starts with a basic set of assumptions. Why you believe what you believe is an expression of your faith. When you take full responsibility for your obligations and personal choices based on your faith, it is called self-government.

Because self-government is a foundational step up from poverty, our nation must revisit its concepts and boundaries. Self-government should be a topic woven into every discussion regarding welfare and poverty. When a nation allows its people the freedom to self-govern, the poor of that nation will have the liberty to activate their faith and work towards self-fulfillment.

A valid family formation is essential to self-governing. Family is the institution through which we learn and pass down values and rules. The family unit provides the basic structure and environment for our faith to flourish. It is the framework that governs us as we grow—body, soul, and spirit. These are all functions of family. Without a proper structure the family becomes a dysfunctional breeding ground for hopelessness. Homosexual activists, militant feminists, and many Left-wing politicians would have you believe that family is any group of people living together in the same dwelling. As many a battered child might tell you if they could, the quality of life in a family has little to do with its descriptive label.

Some say family values can never be defined. Anyone who tries to do so is branded as phobic. The attempt of the lewd Left to redefine family is a planned assault by activists whose beliefs are in direct conflict with the proper structure of family. The only honest basis for their fluid interpretation is that it seems right to them. Major companies and organizations including Catholic charities have been forced to offer domestic partner benefits in order to receive city grants or contracts. In fact, at many corporations, your adult children living at home would not qualify to receive health benefits under your policy even as domestic partners would. Once the standard structure of family is put to a vote, the door for deviancy swings wide open.

The only definition of family that has been able to stand the test of time is the covenant joining of individuals through blood, marriage, or adoption. Those who are serious about leaving or fighting poverty must stand against the liberal forces that would redefine this proper structure. Family is where you first learn about financial stewardship and sexual restraint. It is the work of moms and dads to teach their children compassion, integrity, righteousness, obedience, respect, honor, and love. A traditional family structure offers the best environment through which to identify life's meaning and purpose, hone vocational talents, and develop a work ethic that defeats poverty.

More than the lack of cash, poverty is a state of mind. Success is wealth beyond your imagination. Success is not the winning of a game played with bank accounts, status symbols, and widgets. Dying with the most toys does not make you the winner. Dying with a great financial portfolio does not make your life a success. To live strong and prosperous requires the wisdom to identify your providential call and master it in profession. That is why education should not be confined to one-size-fits-all government institutions. Talents and gifts are unique and individual. They are not equal and are sometimes perceived as unfair or discriminatory. Some talents will lead to a profession that has great financial rewards. Others have great eternal significance but offer limited monetary gains. Left up to the government, anyone trying to exercise these God-given talents and gifts might be declared a bigot, running afoul of the Equal Employment Opportunity Commission for racism, sexism, or homophobia.

Many people feel hopeless because of the misconception that money is the bedmate of success. While it is true that money could follow if one is diligent to set goals and is steadfast and faithful to hone and excel in his talent, it is not true that the lack of an abundant bank account means that one has not fulfilled his life's mission. Mother Teresa is a prime example that a secular worldview of success is wrong. She was elevated to sainthood after departure from this life because her tremendous success was too transcendent to reward in any other way. No amount of money could ever approach the value of her professional contributions, a concept she clearly understood and therefore left the things of this world behind. Acquisitiveness has fed the misconception that living with less means living without value, driving too many to call life a "rat race." We have been relegated to an assortment of labels like "white collar" or "blue collar" as if the value of those accomplishing a project is defined by clothing. All you executives out there, imagine what your life would be like without trash collectors.

God distributes talents and provides the safety of family government as the prime environment for the identification of those talents. That is why gathering up a bunch of two-year-olds in a classroom called preschool is all too often counterproductive and even destructive to the child. Schooling is secondary to parenting. Even a newborn's disposition can be discerned when a loving mother attentively nurtures his development. One Jewish custom is to wait eight days before naming a male child to discern his destined purpose and profession, which the child's name would often reflect. The family then channeled the energy and training of that child towards his mission, profession, or life's work. To help one perfect his talent, formal education must be for sale on the open market to insure a plethora of selections.

The biblical story of Ruth is a picture of the unforeseen outcomes of hard work. Ruth was first and foremost a servant. She was not handed a position on the board of a Fortune 500 Company. Ruth served her husband until he died, and then she served her mother-in-law. She did not demand guaranteed health and retirement benefits or union wages. Ruth became an immigrant farm worker who gleaned what was left in the fields at night. At the end of the day, Ruth's hard work rewarded her with a wonderful and prosperous marriage, many great-grandchildren, including King David, and the honor of being one of only five women listed in the genealogy of Jesus Christ found in the gospel of Matthew.

Vocational government offers great rewards to everyone that willingly, sacrificially, and heartily sets his hands to complete every task with excellence. If you wait for the perfect boss before you put forth your best effort, you will wait forever. If you need a top salary before you will work harder than the person above you, your need will always remain. If you demand a bigger home before you will clean the one you are in, your children will not learn the value of work. Work provides benefits, and how hard it seems is merely a state of mind. Parents who do not require household chores of their children rob them of some eternal lessons about hard work. The people who truly understand why we work are the ones who will never work too hard or live in poverty. A wise philosopher said that true wealth (success) is contentment with one's portion (lot in life).

The hope of the poor is not found on Uncle Sam's plantation. It's found in an attitude change, one that is optimistic and forward-thinking. Hope is found in strong moral and ethical standards. Hope is found in knowing our history and not allowing poverty pimps to manipulate our past to their benefit. Hope is found in heartfelt, genuine charity and in durable marriages and families. Hope is found in people exercising their God-given talents and gifts in the marketplace, unencumbered by excessive taxation and regulations. Hope is found in the free movement of capital and in ridding our land of poisonous ideas, such as multiculturalism, and scrapping failed programs, such as our current welfare system. More than those, however, hope is found in the hearts of any and every American who makes the conscious decision to leave poverty and strive for something greater.

It can be done, and if we are to live up to the potential and promise of this nation, it must be done.

Acknowledgments

I thank the Lord for all of my supporters and take this opportunity to acknowledge a few special friends that helped make this book a reality.

My friend and fellow warrior Joseph Farah; my brilliant and thought-provoking editor Joel Miller; the entire staff of WND Books and Thomas Nelson; my dear friend and sounding board Bob Borens; my comrade and exceptional external affairs director Telly Lovelace; my very creative and luminous writer/editor David Hodel; my fantastic (and smart) writing assistants Phillip Johnson, Victor Conkle, and Joel Mowbray; and my resilient and faithful staff, Keisha Coleman, Timothy McGhee, Jermil Outlaw, and Paula Clemmer.

Also many thanks and blessings to my extraordinary family, Essie, Avis, Michael, Vera, Eric; Eric N., Angel N., and my beautiful and beloved Rachel (1988–2003); also to my wonderful friends, Randy and Betty Adler, Doug and Karen Kessler, Dan and Priscilla Sharp, Steve and Marie Madison, Barry and Bridget Conner, John and Tricia Uhlmann, and Fred and Ruth Sacher.

Certainly I must mention all of my CURE supporters. Oops, if I attempted to give each of you your due props, I would have no room for the contents of this book! But know that I love you and appreciate all that you have done to help me get the truth out about poverty.

Index

Big Business, 158, 164, 172
bigotry, 41
Birth Control Review, 110
Bolick, Clint, 149
Brown v. Board of Education, 144
bureaucracy, 80, 177, 194
Bush, George W., 6, 24, 125, 148,
  163-64, 195, 198-200

C
Caesar, Shirley, 47
capital gains, 156, 161-64
capitalism, 5, 18, 25, 58-59, 65, 71,
  156, 158-59, 177, 207, 215
Catholic Charities, 216
Cato Institute, 79, 167, 206
Census Bureau, 5, 66, 115, 125-26,
  132, 171
Centers for Disease Control, 136
Chamberlain, Wilt, 116
character building, 138, 141
Charitable Choice, 194-95, 197-98
childcare, 23, 25, 43, 48, 72, 78,
  82-83, 133
Child Nutrition Act, 82
children, 2-3, 18-19, 22-23, 25, 27-
  29, 33, 37, 43, 50, 57, 66, 78-80,
  82-85, 89-90, 94, 96, 101, 106,
  110, 114-17, 122, 125, 129-34,
  136-39, 141-42, 144-51, 153, 172,
  191, 201-5, 207, 210, 212-13,
  216, 218-19
Chilton, David, 176
chlamydia, 125, 136
Christianity, 176, 188
church, 2, 6, 9, 12, 14-15, 33, 41,
  47, 49-50, 61, 63, 72, 84, 86, 90,
  92-93, 101, 110, 112, 137, 184,
  195-96, 198-99, 201, 204, 207,
  210-14
civil rights
  Act, 70, 102

movement, 40, 62-68, 92, 133,
  142, 145
leaders, 27, 64-65, 113
legislation, 50, 56
Civil War, 57
Clinton, Bill, 6, 79, 111, 117, 122,
  164
Clinton, Hillary, 105, 123
Coalition on Urban Renewal and
  Education (CURE), 14-15, 51,
  115, 133, 169, 221
Coles School of Business, 170
Commerce, Department of, 215
compassion, 4, 22, 53, 59, 62, 72,
  76-77, 88, 91, 196, 205, 216
condoms, 23, 50, 89, 135-36, 150
Confederates, 60
Congressional Black Caucus, 111,
  117, 133, 171
Congressional Budget Office, 175
Cornell Review, 106
Corporate America, 56, 142, 159
crime, 5, 12, 29, 34, 41, 62, 85, 94,
  102, 110, 112, 114-115, 122-24,
  132, 154, 160, 190-91, 199, 213

D
Danko, William D., 118
Davis-Bacon Act, 173, 175
death, dying, 3, 28, 29, 40, 49, 62,
  65, 67, 72, 77, 112, 115, 134,
  137, 143, 147-50, 156-57, 161,
  168
death tax, 156, 168-72
deficits, 162
Democrats, Democratic party, 68,
  92, 112, 122, 158
discrimination, 60, 62, 66, 70, 102,
  129, 149, 174, 182-83, 188, 195,
  202, 213
dividend income, 164
Doe v. Bolton, 103

liberal, 5-6, 20, 25, 42, 50, 52, 55-
56, 64, 66-69, 72, 75, 77, 79, 82,
87-88, 90-91, 93-94, 96-97, 101-3,
106, 110, 112, 117-19, 126, 132-
33, 135, 138-40, 144, 147, 150,
156, 158, 161-63, 168, 170, 173,
176, 182, 187-88, 190-91, 199,
204, 215-16
Liddy, G. Gordon, 178
Lincoln, President Abraham, 154
literacy, 25, 77, 79
livable wage, 3, 10-11, 42, 95, 121
lynching, 61, 63, 65, 183

M
Malcolm X, 67
marriage, 18, 23, 25-26, 36, 48, 66,
76, 90-91, 95, 100-1, 104-7, 114-
16, 120, 123, 127, 130, 132-33,
139, 187, 200, 212, 216, 218-19
Marx, Karl, 86
McClain, Shirley, 93
McKinney, Cynthia, 186
McWhorter, John, 145
Medical Savings Accounts, 178
Medicaid, 2, 30, 33-35, 83, 155
Medicare, 2, 70, 83, 166-67, 178
Mencken, H. L., 127
military, blacks in, 40, 44, 62-63,
126, 134, 144
minimum wage, 8, 10, 43, 48, 92,
125, 156, 172-73
minority, minorities, 10, 55, 92-93,
95-96, 109, 111, 124, 144-45,
170, 174-75, 181-82, 191, 195,
205
Missouri Compromise, 112
Moore, Steve, 164
Morrison, Toni, 117
Moynihan, Sen. Daniel Patrick,
129, 133
Muhammad, John Allen, 190

multiculturalism, 144, 186-90, 193-
94, 207, 219

N
NAACP, 15, 110, 121, 133
National Center for Policy
Analysis, 132
National Taxpayers Union (NTU),
163, 165
Negro Family, The, 129
Negro Project, 67
Netanyahu, Benjamin, 51
New Deal, 63, 80, 155-56
Newton, Huey, 67
Nissan Corporation, 55-56, 66
Nixon, Richard, 211
No Child Left Behind (NCLB), 148,
151

O
Old Age Survivors and Disability
Insurance (OASDI), 166-67
Oden, Thomas, 188
Other People's Money (OPM),
153-54, 159
out-of-wedlock births, 114, 133
Oval Office, 117

P
Pack, Juluette Bartlett, 111
partial birth abortion, 111-12
Parks, Rosa, 40, 62
payroll taxes, 3, 165-67
pedophilia, 88
Penn State, 94
personal retirement accounts, 207
Planned Parenthood, 108-9, 111,
113
Plessy v. Ferguson, 60
plunder, 159-60
pluralism, 119, 188
politicians, 4-5, 7, 14, 20, 26-27,

94, 100, 104, 111-112, 117, 125-
26, 142-43, 154, 159, 182-83,
185, 191, 214-15
social engineers, 5, 23, 67, 69,
187
Social Security, 2-4, 19, 52, 60, 79-
80, 83, 92, 161, 166-67, 178, 186,
205-7
Special Supplemental Food
Program for Women, Infants,
and Children (WIC), 82
Sproul, R.C., 72
Standard and Poor's, 164
Stanley, Dr. Thomas J., 118
statism, 72, 93
suicide, 29, 92, 108, 207
Supreme Court, 29, 60, 103, 112,
124, 189
syphilis, 67, 116, 135

T
Tanner, Michael, 79, 83
taxes, taxation, 4-7, 10-11, 17-18,
20, 22, 25, 29-30, 36, 43, 58, 70,
73, 95-96, 108, 122, 131, 154-59,
161, 172, 175-76, 178, 183, 196,
198-99, 203, 219
capital gains, 156, 161-64
corporate income, 156, 158-59,
165, 173
death, estate, 57, 156, 168-72
payroll, 2-3, 165-68, 205, 207
Temporary Assistance for Needy
Families (TANF), 78-83
Ten Commandments, 91, 204
Three Strikes, 124
Till, Emmett, 62
Title X, 135-36
treasury, 160
Truth, Sojourner, 113
Tubman, Harriet, 113
Tuskegee Project, 67

U
Uncle Sam, 59, 72-73, 78, 80, 84,
87, 94, 99, 114, 116, 119-21, 129,
133, 135, 137, 141-42, 146-47,
154-55, 158-59, 164, 168-69, 172,
174, 176-77, 196, 200, 213-14
Uncle Sam's Plantation, 49, 69, 78,
92, 97, 99, 104, 118, 186, 219
Uncle Tom, 28, 73
underclass, 4, 117
unemployment, 11, 34, 60, 121,
129, 167, 172
United States Congress, 185
University of Chicago, 108
University of Massachusetts, 100
University of Michigan, 189, 191
University of North Carolina,
Chapel Hill, 71
Urban League, The, 121
USA Today, 214

V
Vazonyi, Balint, 69
venture capital, 157
Viacom, 157
victimology, 77, 145

W
wage laws, 10, 156, 172-73
wages
minimum, 8, 10, 43, 48, 92, 125,
156, 172-73
"living", 156, 173
Waters, Maxine, 66, 122, 186
Watts, Rep. J.C., 171
Welfare Reform Act of 1996, 79
welfare-to-work, 80
Wellesley College, 105
West, Cornell, 186
WIC—see Special Supplemental
Food Program for Women,
Infants, and Children (WIC)

Also from WND BOOKS

For over a hundred years, the *New York Times* has purported to present straight news and hard facts. But, as Bob Kohn shows in *Journalistic Fraud*, the founders' original vision has been hijacked, and today, instead of straight news readers are given mere editorial under the pretense of objective journalism. Kohn, a lifelong reader of the *Times*, shows point by point the methods by which the *Times'* mission has been subverted by the present management and how such fraudulence directly corrupts hundreds of news agencies across the world. ISBN 0-7852-6104-4

The Savage Nation: Saving America from the Liberal Assault on our Borders, Language, and Culture warns that our country is losing its identity and becoming a victim of political correctness, unmonitored immigration, and socialistic ideals. Michael Savage, whose program is the fourth-largest radio talk show and is heard on more than three hundred stations coast to coast, uses bold, biting, and hilarious straight talk to take aim at the sacred cows of our ever-eroding culture and wages war against the "group of psychopaths" known as PETA, the ACLU, and the liberal media. ISBN 0-7852-6353-5

Breach of Trust is Tom Cobum's gripping story of how he and other Republican revolutionaries took Congress by storm as part of the historic Class of '94, tried to wrest control from the hands of career politicians and push forward with legislation that would dramatically limit the size and scope of government, but found that Washington awas unwilling to change. ISBN 0-7852-6220-2

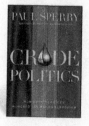

In *Crude Politics*, WorldNetDaily.com's Washington bureau chief Paul Sperry presents alarming evidence that the Bush administration diplomats resumed talks with Pakistani officials over a gas and oil pipeline in Afghanistan while the United States was still reeling from the horror of September 11, 2001. Paul Sperry contends that, true to America's foreign policy of the last century, the Bush administration seized the opportunity to use the attacks as reason to oust the Taliban—the major obstacle blocking plans for the pipeline. ISBN 0-7852-6271-7

WHISTLEBLOWER MAGAZINE

The Internet's leading independent English-language news site, WorldNetDaily.com, has an amazing sister publication. It's called Whistleblower. This monthly print magazine—described by one prominent reviewer as "printed lightning, searing the facts about important current issues into your brain with the force of a thunderclap"—is very different from other news publications.

Each and every issue is a truly groundbreaking, insightful special report on a single topic of great importance—a topic generally ignored by the rest of the news media, such as: the income tax, guns in America, the deliberate dumbing-down of American education, the radical Islamic threat to America, Christian persecution worldwide, the war between Evolution and Intelligent Design, and the radical environmental movement.

You can subscribe to Whistleblower for only $39.95 (and save $50 off the single-copy price!) by calling toll-free 1-800-4-WND-COM (1-800-496-3266) or by logging on to WorldNetDaily.com's online store, ShopNetDaily.com.